$15.

100 Years of Collecting in America
The Story of Sotheby Parke Bernet

100 Years of Collecting in America

The Story of Sotheby Parke Bernet

By Thomas E. Norton
Foreword by Douglas Dillon

Harry N. Abrams, Inc., Publishers, New York

Project Director: Margaret L. Kaplan
Editor: Ellyn Childs Allison
Designer: Tina Davis Snyder
Photo Editor: Barbara Lyons

ISBN 0-8109-1615-0
ISBN 0-8109-2291-6 (pbk.)
Library of Congress Catalog Card Number: 84-71318

Printed and bound in Italy

Foreword

The history of fine art auctions in America is an indelible record of public opinion in the realm of aesthetics and taste. In every auction, the work of art that has the greatest appeal commands the highest price, and a reading of the roster of objects and artists most frequently selected gives a clear and fascinating picture of the evolution of fashion and taste in America.

The history of Sotheby Parke Bernet and its predecessor firms in America gives us a quick synopsis of where we were and how we have changed and how much we enjoyed ourselves in the process. Looking at the many illustrations of works of art sold over the course of a century, we are mesmerized by the range of objects that have passed through their auction rooms.

The days when America's cultural resources were sparse and neglected now seem remote, but nearly all of the great collections that we enjoy today were created by just three or four generations of Americans over the last one hundred years. Never before has any nation collected with such an appetite or on such a scale, and the pace seems to accelerate each year. New museums are being built in every state in the nation, established museums continue to expand, and individual collectors spend enormous sums for the work of artists who were unknown just a short time ago.

Auctions play a crucial role in the process of building the outstanding private collections that form the basis of our great museums. As is fitting in a democracy, auctions are open to all, and the only rules are the basic laws of economics. Although record prices catch the headlines and the cost of many objects may be prohibitive, the history recorded here shows that connoisseurship is much more important than a vast fortune to those who would succeed at auction.

I have had the great pleasure of living in a period that can be seen as a golden age for collecting in America. For the past fifteen years, I have been privileged to watch at close range the remarkable growth in the collections of the Metropolitan Museum of Art. I myself have enjoyed collecting and like many others have lamented the scarcity of first-rate material on the market in one category or another. That has almost always been the case. Because serious collectors set exacting standards, they must expect the chase to be difficult. Still, there is always hope, and new prizes continue to appear at auction. This book is the history of an institution that has had a marvelous collaboration with the collectors of our past and, with the coming generation of collectors, looks forward to an even more exciting future.

DOUGLAS DILLON

Preface and Acknowledgments

Auctioneers are by nature and training inveterate optimists who are always looking toward the future. What happened a week, or a month, or a year ago is not as interesting to them as next week's, or next month's, or next year's sales. Thus, despite a wealth of catalogues—some with prices, many without—in the company's archives and in the major public reference libraries, I must concur with Frank Herrmann, author of *Sotheby's: Portrait of an Auction House,* that "inevitably, very little is known about the firm's earliest days." Herrmann's chronicle, like Wesley Towner's *The Elegant Auctioneers,* recounts in as much detail as possible the history of Parke-Bernet Galleries and Sotheby's, with an account of the personalities, crises, and triumphs that shaped the firm through the years. The aim of this volume is different: it is to provide a pictorial record of some of the most intriguing, typical, sensational, unusual, and expensive objects sold by the firm during the past one hundred years.

Obviously, no selection would have pleased everybody. Nor could I hope to give full coverage to all of the many fields of collecting. Had I a second volume, I would devote more attention to modern and contemporary art and to the various applied arts. The chronological format of the book and the practical aspects of photograph availability also necessitated some compromises, as did my desire to describe the scholarly and historical aspects of collecting in order to give depth to the visual record.

I hope that readers will enjoy this kaleidoscopic review of a century of collecting in America and come away with a heightened appreciation of the role of the auction house in the context of American social, economic, and artistic history—and more specifically of the place that Sotheby Parke Bernet and its ancestors have held in the cultural life of New York City.

The directors and staff of Sotheby's were enormously helpful during every phase of my attempt to compile this overview of one hundred years of collecting and of auctions. I am especially grateful to the following people, who spent hours hunting down needles in the haystack and expediting the book's production: Sandy Carroll, Leslie Keno, Rose Kissel, James Lally, Rosalyn Narbutas, Pamela Pinto, Elizabeth Robbins, Elizabeth White, and David Wille—all of Sotheby's. My warm thanks are also due to Cathy McCarty, who performed incredible feats of organization during the initial phases of research.

Other individuals who were both encouraging and generous with their time and knowledge include Alexander Acevedo, Brenda Auslander, Edward Lee Cave, Mark Cooper, Dr. William Gerdts, Dr. Susan Hobbs, Judith Landrigan, Jerry E. Patterson, Betsy Pinover, Dennis Scioli, Richard Wunder, and Eric M. Zafran.

The staffs of the New York Public Library, of the New-York Historical Society's library, of the Frick Art Reference Library, and of the American Antiquarian Society have all been patient and cooperative.

My thanks to all of the above and the many others too numerous to mention who have borne with me during the compilation, writing, and production of this book.

THOMAS E. NORTON

Above: An early picture auction, New York, 1875.

Below: Sotheby's main auction room at 1334 York Avenue during the auction of Degas's *L'Attente* from the Havemeyer collection on May 18, 1983. In the rostrum is the president of Sotheby's in America, John L. Marion.

Introduction

It is just before the scheduled sale time and the discreetly well-dressed patrons are arriving in their chauffeured vehicles or honking taxis or on foot. All seem to converge at once on the entrance for the evening's events. To professionals and dedicated amateurs alike, this is an experience more exhilarating than anything a gambling casino can provide. This is the "big time": a major auction of works of art held at the New York galleries of Sotheby Parke Bernet—the leading international auctioneers.

After receiving worldwide attention and careful scrutiny, after being photographed and tested and evaluated and catalogued and publicized, treasures from a well-known collection are to be offered and sold, one by one, to the highest bidder. The stakes are high; the prizes unique; the tension almost unbearable. An electrically charged atmosphere pervades the familiar arena as old friends greet each other warmly but warily while obvious rivals nod to each other with feigned cordiality.

It's everyone for himself, since all are potential competitors for the same objects on offer. Dealers arrive with well-worn catalogues clutched to their sides and mysterious new clients in tow. Colleagues wonder whether the newcomers will be steadfast rivals or turn out to be—as do most people in the crowded room—just curious observers who attend these tribal rites of the rich and powerful to see and be seen and to take the pulse of the market.

The din grows louder as everyone makes a last-minute effort to find out who's after what and how much this or that will go for. The scramble for seats is still in progress when the auctioneer steps into the rostrum to quiet the crowd and begin the evening's business.

As the sale progresses according to time-honored rituals, a special ambience begins to envelop the auction room, changing subtly as each lot is hammered down—sometimes after heated competition from enthusiastic contenders, at other times after less frenzied bidding from bargain-seekers, or—worse yet—a loud silence that indicates failure to find a buyer at any price. Often a power struggle develops that ends only when the bidder with both the requisite funds *and* the strongest urge to possess something outbids all rivals and captures the prize. If there is applause, it is often as much in appreciation of a bidder's courage and determination as it is in recognition of the specialness of the object itself or its high price.

There are any number of reasons—death and taxes being two of the more widely recognized—why people dispose of their valued possessions. Whatever the reason, a means must exist for bringing sellers and buyers together, and this is what the business of auctions is all about.

Auctioneering must be among civilization's oldest professions. When the first organized societies realized the need for a more efficient method of redistributing surplus commodities than autocratic whim or face-to-face haggling, auctions developed. Society realized the importance of the auction as an efficient means for buyers and sellers to come to agreement. The method proved useful for the redistribution of mundane goods such as fish and corn, as well as for scarce or unique or precious commodities such as works of art, thoroughbred horses, and gems.

Art collecting, art dealing, and art auctions are known to have been commonplace in ancient Rome, a city that perhaps carried the auction system to excessive lengths. The entire Roman Empire (meaning the civilized world) was sold at an auction conducted by the Praetorian Guard, who had seized power by assassinating the duly-elected ruler, Emperor Pertinax, in A.D. 193. A wealthy senator, Marcus Didius Julianus, made the winning bid and was immediately proclaimed emperor. Unluckily for him, his sixty-six-day reign ended with his public beheading.

There was certainly at least limited art trading and auctioning during the Renaissance in Europe, but it was the rise of a prosperous middle class in the newly rich mercantile society of the Netherlands during the seventeenth century that brought about the art market—with specialized art auctions—in a form that directly anticipates our own situation today.

In the eighteenth century, the London and Paris art markets became highly organized in response to the emerging wealth and taste for collecting among the prosperous middle class. Sotheby's in London dates back to 1744.

In the wake of the French Revolution and the subsequent turmoil on the Continent, London, rich from shipping and new industry, became the center of the art market.

Toward the end of the nineteenth century, similar conditions made New York the heir to London as it in turn became the center of a huge industrial empire. Wealth flowed into the city and some of it was spent on luxury goods, including fine art and antiques. A new, upwardly mobile society with the time, money, and interest began to collect and soon required an auction firm that could adequately serve its needs.

Collecting on a smaller scale had of course started earlier in the United States, and auctions of art objects are recorded as early as 1785, when one Pierre Eugène de Simitière sold the contents of his "American Museum" in Philadelphia. In Boston, in 1820, an auctioneer announced the dispersal of a "Gallery of. . . original cabinet paintings, being a truly splendid and valuable collection, selected with great care and expense from the various cabinets of Rome, Naples, Florence, Amsterdam, Paris, and London. Comprising the works of the Great Masters from the fourteenth century to the present time, the whole in elegant frames."

But it was in New York City that art patronage, art collecting, and art auctions achieved major attention as the metropolis waxed rich on the trade that went through its port as well as on the enormous industrial activity fueled by cheap immigrant labor. One of New York's most distinguished mayors, Philip Hone (1780–1851), made his fortune as an auctioneer—a fortune which afforded him the luxuries of politics and art collecting as well as the leisure time to keep a detailed diary of his activities during these exciting years when New York was outdistancing its rivals, Boston and Philadelphia.

New York: 1883

By 1883 New York was something of a boom town. Old money, new money, vast building schemes, and an exploding population characterized the city. Its 1.3 million inhabitants were almost evenly divided between the native-born and immigrants. In May the "Great East River Bridge" linking the then independent cities of Brooklyn and New York was inaugurated. It was the world's longest span and its completion gave New Yorkers—even the poorest recent arrivals—a great sense of accomplishment and pride. In October the Metropolitan Opera House opened with a gala performance of Gounod's *Faust*. Mansions were rising along Fifth Avenue's upper reaches, where uptown on the park the Metropolitan Museum had found its home, and for those who complained about the high cost of owning a house in Manhattan there were elegant "French flats" (better known as apartment houses) such as the Dakota or the Chelsea available for rental or cooperative ownership. Contemporary European, especially French, paintings were for sale at Knoedler's, Goupil's, and other dealers' establishments, and on East Twenty-third Street, at Madison Square, a new organization called the American Art Association first opened its doors to the public.

Madison Square a century ago was the center of an extraordinarily diverse neighborhood, even by New York standards. Grand hotels, elegant mansions, undistinguished brownstones, stores, and commercial establishments of every

In 1883, the year the American Art Association set up shop on Madison Square, John A. Roebling's great suspension bridge was opened to traffic between New York and Brooklyn, and citizens on both banks of the East River rejoiced.

New York's Metropolitan Opera House opened in 1883 on Broadway between Thirty-ninth and Fortieth streets. It was demolished in 1966, and the Opera moved uptown to Lincoln Center.

The first address of the American Art Association was 6–8 East Twenty-third Street, New York City—on Madison Square, in the Kurtz Photographic Gallery building.

In the 1880s, when this photograph was taken, the National Academy of Design was located on Fourth Avenue, just down the street from the American Art Association. It was to this building that the landmark Impressionist exhibition of 1886 was removed after a stormy debut at the Association's galleries.

description existed side by side. The old railroad terminal at Twenty-sixth Street had been transformed into an entertainment center by P. T. Barnum (it would later be renamed Madison Square Garden and in 1889 would be razed to make way for Stanford White's magnificent new Madison Square Garden). The National Academy was ensconced in its Venetian palazzo at Twenty-third Street and Fourth Avenue, while on the other side of the Square, the Eden Musée, renowned for its waxworks, attracted thousands. Bouguereau's *Satyr and Nymphs,* hanging over the ornate bar of the celebrated Hoffman House nearby, titillated the gentlemen and scandalized the ladies who patronized the hotel.

The American Art Association

It was in this neighborhood then, where Theodore Roosevelt had been born in 1858 and Edith Wharton in 1862, that, according to the chief chronicler of New York, A. P. Stokes, "the American Art Association [was] formed by James F. Sutton, R. Austin Robertson, and Thomas E. Kirby, for the encouragement and promotion of American Art....It possessed the lease of The American Art Gallery, consisting of a room 46′ x 36′, with adjoining offices, in the building of Wm. Kurtz, a photographer, at 6–8 East Twenty-third Street....The business of the Association is the exhibition and sale of works of art and literature." Thus the understated announcement of the formation of what would eventually become New York's—and America's—foremost marketplace for sales of fine art, antiques, rare books and prints, jewelry, and that vast grouping of miscellaneous objects now included under the heading "collectibles."

The three co-founders were not exactly strangers to the ways of New York's burgeoning art trade. James Fountain Sutton, a rich admirer of contemporary painting and Oriental ceramics, was a son-in-law of Rowland H. Macy, whose "cash-only" dry-goods establishment had developed into a mighty department store. Sutton's previous attempts at retailing art in his "American Art Gallery" had not been a commercial success, even though he was well supplied with the latest in Chinese curios and artifacts imported by his colleague, the second member of the American Art Association triumvirate, R. Austin Robertson.

The magic new ingredient in the mix was the presence of an ambitious and imaginative young auctioneer named Thomas E. Kirby.

The Kirby Years: 1885–1923

At first dedicated exclusively to exhibitions and retail sales, the American Art Association shifted gears somewhat reluctantly in 1885 when, in the aftermath of a general economic downturn, New York's Metropolitan Bank failed and its owner, George I. Seney, was forced by the creditors to liquidate his extensive art collection. Inveterate auctioneer Kirby persuaded his partners to undertake the sale of this fine collection in a manner befitting the aims and ideals of their organization. Kirby realized that this was a golden opportunity for the Association to expand the business and at the same time to maintain their respectable and fashionable image by managing the auction as an important artistic, cultural, and social event far removed from the often questionable and shoddy practices of most auctioneers in the city at that time. The sale was a triumph, and the manner in which Kirby and his partners handled the exhibition, catalogue, publicity, and auction was widely acclaimed.

This success changed the destiny of the firm and, indeed, the way all such auctions would be conducted in the future. Other public sales soon followed: in the autumn of 1885 the George Whitney collection of paintings, and in 1886 the Mary Jane Morgan sale of 2,628 lots of pictures, porcelains, and other treasures from her house on Madison Square.

In 1887 the disposal of the contents of A. T. Stewart's mansion and in 1889 the sale of the collection of Don Pedro de Borbón helped to identify the American Art Association in the public mind with the management of important auctions.

By 1892 R. Austin Robertson had retired from the firm, and in 1895 James F. Sutton withdrew from active participation. Kirby and his auctions had won the day, but not before two of the most important special exhibitions ever held in America were orchestrated by Sutton at the gallery on East Twenty-third Street: the first French Impressionist show in America in 1886 and the Millet/Barye exhibition of 1889–90. Both were to have far-reaching effects on American taste and collecting habits.

Kirby, assisted by Rose Lorenz, who masterminded the exhibitions and catalogues, dominated the American art auction scene for forty years. As the managers of virtually every important art auction held in America for decades, the American Art Association prospered and collectors and dealers benefited from the high standards, informative catalogues, and attractively arranged pre-sale exhibitions that became synonymous with the firm.

At first the major auctions were held at Chickering Hall, an auditorium at Fifth Avenue and Eighteenth Street, while ordinary sales were held on the Association's premises at East Twenty-third Street. Then, as the city moved its commercial and residential center northward, important sales began to be held at Mendelssohn Hall, at Broadway and Fortieth Street. This auditorium was right in the heart of the notorious "Tenderloin" district, and for the auction of Mrs. S. D. Warren's collection of Barbizon paintings in 1903, a policeman was assigned to protect the elegant auction-goers from the unsavory characters who frequented the area. A few years later the big sales were conducted at the new Plaza Hotel on Fifth Avenue at Central Park South, following the northerly trend of the fashionable city.

In 1922, as the area around Madison Square became more commercial and with the Flatiron Building now dominating the skyline, it was decided to abandon the old Twenty-third Street location and move uptown to Madison Avenue and Fifty-seventh Street. There an elegant, Renaissance-style palazzo was built especially for the firm. It was the end of the Kirby era. During these first forty years some $60 million worth of art and antiques, jewels, and rare books had been sold to an ever-growing audience of dealers and collectors, and the foundations had been laid for the future course of the American Art Association and its successors.

Thomas E. Kirby at seventy-five. Under his direction, the American Art Association became the principal art auction house in the United States.

The Bishop Era: 1923–1937

The new owner of the American Art Association was Cortlandt Field Bishop, a wealthy and socially prominent collector. It was under Bishop that Hiram Parke, Otto Bernet, and their colleagues built on the strengths of the Kirby tradition and expanded the nation's premier auction facility for art, antiques, and books.

However, there was more competition now for the title of premier auction facility, and the most persistent contender was the Anderson Galleries, originally a small book auction firm but since 1917 an aggressive company selling art and antiques as well as books and prints. That year the Anderson Galleries had moved into the ornate and conveniently located former headquarters of the Arion Society, a German social organization which, like so many other German clubs, ceased operations during World War I. The genius behind the "new" Anderson Galleries at Park Avenue and Fifty-ninth Street was Mitchell Kennerly, an amazingly energetic patron of arts and letters—a publisher, bibliophile, and sympathetic friend of modern art and literature. In 1921 Alfred Stieglitz held a successful one-man show of his photographs at Kennerly's Anderson Galleries, and in that same year the American painter Marsden Hartley sold a number of his canvases there at auction. In 1925 Stieglitz opened his Intimate Gallery in one of the Anderson Galleries' rooms, and it was here that Georgia O'Keeffe, Charles Demuth, John Marin, and other young artists in the Stieglitz stable were able to show their work.

Several important art sales were taken away from the American Art Association by the Anderson Galleries, most notably the Viscount Leverhulme auction of 1926, and even though these were the boom years of the 1920s, with more and bigger sales at constantly escalating prices, the competition hurt.

After a few years Bishop had seen enough to realize that his best course was to buy out the competition. Accordingly, in 1927 he paid $417,500 for the Anderson Galleries. The two firms continued in their separate locations for two years, but in 1929 they formally merged and marched forward under the unwieldy corporate title: "American Art Association–Anderson Galleries, Inc." The building at 489 Park Avenue was closed and the combined operation opened the new season at 30 East Fifty-seventh Street.

The prosperity of the 1920s fueled a boom in collecting—not just the traditional Barbizon pictures and Italian antiques favored by the previous generation but all sorts of new things as well. Modern painting was becoming more acceptable, decorative arts of the eighteenth century enjoyed a tremendous vogue, and an energetic group of wealthy collectors was responsible for organizing a memorable exhibition of American antique furniture at the American Art Association–Anderson Galleries in the fall of 1929—the famous Girl Scout Exhibition.

But despite good sales, an expanding market, and many triumphs, things did not go as smoothly as Bishop might have wished. In addition to the problems created by his own capricious and highhanded direction, there were conflicts between rival managements from the formerly separate companies. Much worse, the Great Depression, with its ever-widening effects, wreaked havoc on the art auction market.

By 1935, when Bishop died, the firm was in poor financial shape even though Parke and Bernet still enjoyed the loyal following of their colleagues, the art trade, and the collectors who patronized the American Art Association–Anderson Galleries auctions.

In 1937, when Bishop's widow sought to bring Kennerly out of retirement to run things, Parke and Bernet and the entire expert and managerial staff left *en masse* to form a new company.

The A. T. Stewart mansion, on Fifth Avenue at Thirty-fourth Street, one of the city's most grandiose structures.

Below: A reception for the press was held on December 21, 1884, in the art gallery of the Vanderbilt mansion in New York City, between Fifty-first and Fifty-second streets. Three years later, Cornelius Vanderbilt purchased Rosa Bonheur's *Horse Fair* at the American Art Association—but not for his gallery. Instead, he presented the splendid painting to the Metropolitan Museum of Art.

In an energetic bid to compete with the American Art Association for the fine-art and antiques market, the Anderson Auction Company moved uptown in 1917 to this building at 489 Park Avenue, on the southeast corner of Fifty-seventh Street.

The second home of the American Art Association was a specially designed building erected in 1922, occupying the block between Fifty-sixth and Fifty-seventh streets on the east side of Madison Avenue. From 1939 until 1949, it was the home of Parke-Bernet Galleries, as well.

The American Art Association–Anderson Galleries during the pre-sale exhibition of "One Hundred Important Antiques," a collection of American furniture and decorative arts consigned by the well-known dealer Israel Sack in 1932.

The highest price of the sale was $6,300—for a Goddard-Townsend kneehole desk, made in Newport, Rhode Island, about 1770, which is visible at the left of the photograph.

The Parke-Bernet Years: 1937–1949

In November of 1937, with no capital, no building, and no auctions lined up, the new organization was registered under the name Parke-Bernet Galleries, Inc. In January the firm's first auction was successfully staged in a makeshift gallery at 742 Fifth Avenue (site of the present Van Cleef & Arpels store in the Bergdorf Goodman building) and things were off to a good start.

Hiram Parke, the aristocratic-looking auctioneer and favorite of the carriage trade, had a worthy partner in Otto Bernet, the Swiss-born, hard-working, nuts-and-bolts businessman who took care of daily affairs and made sure things ran as they were supposed to. Complementing this unlikely but remarkably successful pair was an assortment of talented colleagues who provided the firm with depth and breadth. There was Arthur Swann, the English-born dean of American book cataloguers, and his assistant, Anthony Bade, who specialized in rare prints. In charge of cataloguing the art sales was Leslie Hyam, also English-born, who had joined the business in 1924 after attending Cambridge and a brief stint working for Sir Joseph Duveen's brother Charles, who was also an art dealer, though not of Sir Joseph's caliber. Hyam's knowledge of art was largely self-acquired but his brilliance and perseverance won him the respect of knowledgeable people. He carried the tradition of the informative, authoritative catalogue to new heights, while Mary Vandegrift supervised the typography and publication of these much-admired catalogues. Louis Marion, Otto Bernet's protégé and father of John Marion, Sotheby Parke Bernet's president in the seventies and eighties, became business manager and ultimately chief auctioneer.

But that was still in the future. Parke and Bernet, within a year of their departure, had so completely taken over the leadership of the industry that they were able to buy up what was left of the assets and goodwill of their semidefunct parent for a few thousand dollars and move back into the grand old premises at 30 East Fifty-seventh Street.

Parke-Bernet Galleries (usually mistakenly frenchified into "Parke-Burnay") emerged as the country's foremost auctioneer of fine and decorative art, jewelry, and literary property.

Then came the war in Europe and Asia which so devastated the rest of the world that the international art trade virtually ceased to exist. Parke-Bernet, by reason of its location in the world's most affluent city and most stable nation, became the world's most important auction house.

Moreover, the tradition of holding special exhibitions continued, with annual "salons" of contemporary art and an occasional special loan show for a good cause. One of the most spectacular of these benefit exhibitions was that of French furniture and decorative arts held in 1942 under the auspices of the American Women's Volunteer Services. In the years to come the Art Treasures Exhibition held annually by New York's leading dealers at Parke-Bernet became the showcase of the finest in antiques and decorative accessories.

Parke-Bernet Galleries' first location—at 742 Fifth Avenue, on the northwest corner of Fifty-seventh Street.

The New Generation Takes Over: 1949–1963

Otto Bernet died in 1945 and Major Parke (as he preferred to be called, in deference to a brief stint in the Pennsylvania State Militia) retired five years later (he died in 1957). The firm was now in the hands of Leslie Hyam, Mary Vandegrift, and Louis Marion, whose accession to full control coincided with the removal of the firm from Fifty-seventh Street and Madison Avenue, where the premises were to be demolished to make way for a tall office building, to a much more residential neighborhood one mile north, 980 Madison Avenue, between Seventy-sixth and Seventy-seventh streets.

There, opposite the Hotel Carlyle, a sculpture by Wheeler Williams over the main entrance titled *Venus Bringing the Arts to Manhattan* greeted visitors to the new galleries. Sales grew in number and in dollar volume through the triumphant years of the late fifties and early sixties, when the Lurcy and Foy collections, the great Museum of Modern Art Benefit auction, the Streeter book sales, and the fabled Erickson auction of Old Masters made the name Parke-Bernet famous everywhere for its luxurious presentation of the finest property at auction.

But this position of preeminence was not to last forever. With the relaxation of trade restrictions and the new ease of overseas travel, the art market became truly international. British and French auctioneers opened offices in New York, and in 1964, to capitalize on the increased internationality of the art market, Sotheby's, the oldest and largest British auction house, acquired Parke-Bernet, the grande dame of American auction galleries.

The Parke-Bernet building at 980 Madison Avenue was erected in 1949. Another story was added ten years later.

In 1980 Sotheby Parke Bernet moved to a new
location, on East Seventy-second Street.

The Anglo-American Era: 1964–1983

An infusion of talented young Englishmen led by Peregrine Pollen, who served as president of the New York firm from 1965 to 1972, augmented the Parke-Bernet staff, and the firm entered a period of unprecedented growth and expansion. Branch offices were opened, specialized sales increased, imaginative ways of encouraging new young collectors were tried, and the name of Sotheby Parke Bernet became so well known around the world that even natives in remote jungles of Central America, when approached by traders to sell their ancient treasures, are said to have produced Sotheby Parke Bernet catalogues to help them in arriving at a satisfactory price.

During the years of high inflation around the world in the sixties and seventies, the art market exploded. John Marion, president and chief executive since 1972, conducted one record-breaking sale after another. New areas of collecting interest, such as Art Nouveau, Art Deco, Victoriana, and Latin American art, brought more and more people into the auction market. The sales at Sotheby Parke Bernet in New York continually set the pace.

By the end of the 1970s the firm's expanding operations had obviously outgrown the familiar building on Madison Avenue. After a long search a larger building farther east—at Seventy-second Street and York Avenue—was selected. After extensive remodeling, the custom-designed galleries opened in the fall of 1980 and soon became the headquarters of Sotheby Parke Bernet in America.

In September 1983—one hundred years after the founding of the American Art Association—a pivotal event occurred in Sotheby Parke Bernet's history. In a move strongly endorsed by the Board of Directors in London, the company was acquired by A. Alfred Taubman, a leading American businessman, philanthropist, art patron, and collector. A strengthened financial base, enhanced international marketing, expanded client services in real estate and art financing, and a name change on all continents to "Sotheby's" were direct results of private ownership.

Perhaps most significant was the addition of prominent new Board members, such as American industrialists Henry Ford II as Vice Chairman and Max M. Fisher; business leaders and art collectors Baron Thyssen-Bornemisza of Switzerland and Seiji Tsutsumi of Japan; and civic and cultural leader Ann (Mrs. Gordon) Getty. Also appointed to the Board were Emilio Gioia, Alexis Gregory, Carroll (Mrs. Milton) Petrie, all of New York; Earl E. T. Smith of Palm Beach; and Leslie H. Wexner of Ohio.

During the course of the century, fashions in collecting have come and gone and there have been changes in the name, location, ownership, and size of the organization that first began in a modest rented space on East Twenty-third Street. Yet many of the traditions and practices that began there and developed during the firm's earliest years continue to be honored.

Beautifully printed and illustrated catalogues of one-owner collections and multiple-owner specialized sales continue to be published, informing as many potential bidders as possible—seasoned professionals as well as timid neophytes. The pre-sale exhibitions are still carefully arranged in spacious galleries, and direct participation by private collectors in the auction process is encouraged as strongly today as it was then.

This approach, geared to an affluent constituency of self-reliant but not always sophisticated entrepreneurs, was considered radical in the 1880s but has come to be the standard in the international art auction world.

These are the enduring traditions of Sotheby's in America, as heir to the rich histories of ancestor firms that go back a century in New York and some two and one-half centuries in London.

1884

George Inness. *Winter Morning, Montclair.* 1882. Oil on canvas, 30 x 45″. Montclair Art Museum, Montclair, New Jersey. Gift of Mrs. Arthur D. Whiteside, 1961. Number 51 in the Inness Memorial Exhibition held by the American Art Association at their gallery on Madison Square South in April 1884.

The first event to capture the public's attention and attract the right sort of people to the American Art Gallery, newly established at 6–8 East Twenty-third Street, was the "Special Exhibition of Oil Paintings—Works of Mr. George Inness, N.A., including his famous pictures *Niagara Falls* and *Mount Washington.*"

Inness, born in Newburgh, New York, in 1825, had first exhibited at the National Academy of Design in 1844, so he was no stranger to local collectors. It was only in the mid-1870s, however, that he was able to achieve some real success and financial stability when several of New York's most prominent art patrons began making significant purchases. Among these were Thomas B. Clarke and George Ingraham Seney. By 1878 Inness was able to buy a house in the country—in Montclair, New Jersey, at the foothills of the Orange Mountains, a rural community of some 5,000 people, with easy access by train to New York City. Here, Inness was to paint some of his finest pictures, including the *Winter Morning, Montclair* of 1882 that hung with fifty-six other works when the show of 1884 opened on April 10.

Two days later the *New York Tribune* reported, "Not to know Mr. George Inness argues one's self a benighted Philistine as regards our native art; and yet we fancy that the broad range of the artist's powers illustrated in the remarkable exhibition ... will surprise the confidence even of his friends." Noting that the catalogue contained "an unusual amount of reading matter," the critic mentioned several of the pictures, including one titled *The Valley of the Shadow of Death,* indicative of Inness's preoccupation with philosophical/metaphysical studies that often made it difficult for him to deal with everyday matters. Indeed, the catalogue's message from Inness stated flatly: "Having entrusted to the American Art Association all business matters relating to the disposal of my works, hereafter all negotiation for the purchase and exhibition of same will be transacted through them exclusively.... Wishing to be relieved of all business anxiety while pursuing the profession of Art is my sole reason for making the above arrangement so kindly accorded by the gentlemen composing the American Art Association."

Although the show was not an immediate financial success for either the artist or his sponsor, it did serve to sum up all Inness's previous accomplishments and provide him with a more secure position in the collecting community—a position his pictures would hold for many years after his death in 1894.

1885

The Washington Monument is dedicated.

The Mikado by Gilbert and Sullivan is produced in London.

In the history of art collecting in America, the first painter to achieve what we today might call "superstar" status was Jules Breton (1827–1906). During the middle years of the nineteenth century, his idealized depictions of the peasants of Brittany received the warmest critical and popular acclaim in America as well as in his native France, where he was a faithful exhibitor at the annual Paris Salons. William T. Walters of Baltimore, John Taylor Johnston of New York (the first president of the Metropolitan Museum of Art), Henry C. Gibson and George Whitney of Philadelphia, and George Ingraham Seney of Brooklyn were among the pioneer collectors who bought works by Breton, usually through Samuel Putnam Avery—the celebrated connoisseur, agent, patron, and dealer.

Seney, who had risen to be president of the Metropolitan Bank and was well known as a railroad financier by the late 1870s, had amassed an enormous number of "modern" pictures at the height of his financial success. When his bank failed in 1885, the recently formed art collection was ordered to be sold to satisfy the bank's creditors.

Avery, Seney's advisor, decided that R. Austin Robertson's, Thomas E. Kirby's, and James F. Sutton's American Art Association would be the ideal venue for the sale, and when Kirby managed to allay Sutton's reservations about getting involved in the business of auctions, the sale was scheduled to be held at Chickering Hall on March 31 and April 1 and 2. Breton's *Evening in the Hamlet of Finistère,* which a Parisian critic had called "beyond all question, the first among Breton's works . . . even the first in the Salon [of 1882]," was expected to be the highlight of this premier auction managed by the American Art Association. The critic for the *New York Post* was not as impressed. In addition to calling several of Seney's pictures either bad examples or outright forgeries, he termed the Breton "certainly one of the most individual and pathetic of his minor works."

Kirby filed suit for slander, other newspapers picked up the controversy, and people flocked in to see the preview exhibition organized by the new firm. What they saw was a tastefully hung group of paintings, accompanied by an extremely attractive, professionally edited, and highly informative catalogue worthy of the most impressive art exhibit. This was not a mere *auction*—it was an artistic, social, and financial event occurring in a new marketplace.

Police reinforcements were needed to control the crowds and allow the ticket-holding bidders into Chickering Hall on the evening of the auction. Prices were respectably strong and Breton's *Evening in the Hamlet* brought the highest price of the sale—a record that would, however, be toppled in less than a year, when Mary Jane Morgan's Breton painting, *The Communicants,* commanded an even higher figure.

Jules Breton. *Evening in the Hamlet of Finistère.*
1882. Oil on canvas, 37 x 52″. The Paine Art
Center and Arboretum, Oshkosh, Wisconsin.
Gift of Nathan Paine, 1946. Lot 282 in the auction of the George I. Seney collection, managed
by the American Art Association and held at
Chickering Hall, Fifth Avenue and Eighteenth
Street, on March 31 and April 1–2, 1885. The
price was $18,200.

"In my opinion, up to Millet and Jules Breton
there was . . . progress; but to surpass these
two—don't even talk about it" (*The Complete
Letters of Vincent Van Gogh,* illus. ed., 1959, vol.
1, p. 477).

1886

Apache chief Geronimo surrenders, ending the Indian Wars in the American Southwest.

The Statue of Liberty is dedicated.

"Peach-blow" or "peachbloom" pink-glazed porcelain vase. Chinese, reign of Kangxi (1662–1722). Height 8". Walters Art Gallery, Baltimore, Maryland. Lot 341 in the Mary Jane Morgan sale, managed by the American Art Association and held at Chickering Hall on March 3–5 and 8, 1886.

The vase was bought by William T. Walters of Baltimore for $18,000, amid a flurry of speculation and commentary in the New York newspapers. The price was the highest ever fetched for Chinese porcelain and is indicative of the taste of the era. "Peach-blow" entered the vocabulary of thousands who would now buy the peach-blow-type glass bottles (made in New England) that soon became the rage. Today these Chinese wares are referred to as "peachbloom" glazed porcelains.

Jean-Georges Vibert. *The Missionary's Adventures.* c. 1883. Oil on wood panel, 39 x 53". The Metropolitan Museum of Art, New York. Bequest of Collis P. Huntington, 1925. As *The Missionary's Story,* lot 231 in the Mary Jane Morgan collection sale, managed by the American Art Association and held at Chickering Hall on March 3–5 and 8, 1886. It fetched $25,500.

The colorful and technically marvelous paintings of Jean-Georges Vibert (1840–1902) depicting smug, worldly ecclesiastics were favorites among late nineteenth-century collectors. One such work by Vibert, *The Missionary's Adventures,* impressed three such disparate personalities as Marcel Proust, Mary Jane Morgan, and Collis P. Huntington. In Proust's *Remembrance of Things Past,* the Duc de Guermantes, discussing Vibert's sketch of the picture, says: "I'd infinitely prefer to have the little study by M. Vibert.... You can see the man's got wit to his fingertips: that shabby scarecrow of a missionary standing in front of the sleek prelate who is making his dog do tricks, it's a perfect little poem of subtlety, and even profundity."

Mary Jane Morgan, widow of a wealthy New York merchant, fell under Vibert's spell when she paid Knoedler's $12,500 for the oil painting of the same subject. Mrs. Morgan's penchant for paying high prices when she admired something was well known among the city's dealers. Several snide editorials in the *New York Times* questioning the value and merit of her collection—and specifically her "peach-blow" vase—appeared at the time of the pre-sale exhibition of her effects in 1886. When the auction took place, *The Missionary's Story* (as it was called in the catalogue) fetched double what she had paid for it, and the new owner was none other than Collis P. Huntington, one of the "Big Four" California millionaires (the others were Charles Crocker, Leland Stanford, and Mark Hopkins).

Huntington, who personified the era's ruthless business practices, had started to collect on a grand scale, thanks to the influence of his wife, Arabella. A man of few words, he once confessed to Sir Joseph Duveen, the famous dealer, that he had paid $25,000 for a "religious" painting that he spent so much time looking at he didn't have time to look at any of the others in his house. Huntington even recorded his reactions to the Vibert picture, describing the cardinals "dressed in luxury. One... playing with a dog; one asleep... one looking [at the missionary] with that kind of expression saying 'what a fool you are that you should go out and suffer for the human race when we have such a good time at home....' I sometimes sit half an hour looking at that picture." In S. N. Behrman's biography *Duveen,* this anecdote is followed by Oscar Lewis's supposition that Collis P. Huntington, promoter of the Central Pacific Railroad, a onetime shopkeeper who was shunned by polite society, may have identified with the poor missionary and seen his former partners, Crocker, Hopkins, and Stanford, in the self-indulgent prelates!

Today, a century after it was painted, *The Missionary's Adventures* continues to charm those museum-goers who take the time to look for it at the Metropolitan Museum of Art.

James Sutton, one of the three co-founders of the American Art Association, was an early and devoted patron of Claude Monet and his fellow Impressionists. At one time he owned as many as forty paintings by Monet, most of which were sold after his death in 1917 and after his widow's death in 1933.

While on a trip to Paris in 1885, Sutton arranged to have the dealer Paul Durand-Ruel, champion of the group of painters known, at first derisively, as "Impressionists," send over a large group of their works for an exhibition in New York.

On April 10, 1886, an exhibition of 289 "Works in Oil and Pastel by the Impressionists of Paris," the first such show ever held in America, opened "under the management of The American Art Association of the City of New York." The catalogue was not quite up to the sponsor's usual standards (Manet was confused with Monet, Pontoise was misspelled "Poutoise," and Berthe Morisot was listed as "Morizot"), but the introductory essay by Théodore Duret, a respected and sympathetic critic, succeeded in rebutting those who would condemn the works, by anticipating their likely reactions.

The Impressionist seats himself on the bank of a stream...he paints the water sparkling, silvery, with an azure sheen. The wind is stirring; he paints the reflections broken by the ripple...the winter comes, the Impressionist paints the snow...he paints blue shadows. Then the public laughs outright!... The critics shake their fists and cry after the artist, "Communist" and "Wretch." In vain the unhappy Impressionist protests his perfect sincerity. For... [to the public] the Impressionist's work does not look like the work of the painters who went before him. It is different from theirs, therefore it is bad.

Signac, Renoir, Degas, Boudin, Pissarro, and several lesser-known artists were represented in this show, which the *New York Times* dismissed as full of "crude colors." Rhetorically it asked, "Is this Art?" So intensely negative was the reaction in some quarters that the duty-free bond under which the paintings had been admitted to the country was revoked by the customs collector. Rather than pay the 30-percent duty levied on "commercial" exhibitions, the entire show was removed from the American Art Galleries to the National Academy, just down the block at Twenty-third Street and Fourth Avenue, where the pictures were shown until May.

Altogether, only fifteen pictures were sold—to such collectors as W. L. Andrews, W. H. Fuller, Cyrus J. Lawrence, and H. O. Havemeyer—but the seeds had been sown for a full-fledged love affair between the American public and the "Impressionists of Paris" that continues, unabated, to this day.

Edouard Manet. *The Salmon.* 1869. Oil on canvas, 29 x 37″. Shelburne Museum, Shelburne, Vermont. Electra Havemeyer Webb Fund.

This sumptuous still life was acquired from Manet in 1872 by Durand-Ruel; sold to J.-B. Faure, Paris; repurchased by Durand-Ruel and exhibited by him in April 1886 at the American Art Galleries, New York, where it was bought by Mr. and Mrs. H. O. Havemeyer.

Georges Seurat. *Sunday Afternoon on the Island of La Grande-Jatte*. 1884–86. Oil on canvas, 81 x 120⅜″. The Art Institute of Chicago. Helen Bartlett Memorial Collection.

Seurat's masterpiece was exhibited publicly for the first time anywhere at the American Art Galleries in April 1886. *La Grande-Jatte* was the first major picture of Seurat's to incorporate small dots of color into the brushwork.

Claude Monet. *Ice Breaking Up at Vétheuil*. 1881. Oil on canvas, 23½ x 39¼″. Thyssen-Bornemisza Collection, Lugano, Switzerland.

Monet settled at Vétheuil, down the Seine from Argenteuil, in 1878. In the spring of 1880, he executed several depictions of the rapid melting of the river ice after the intensely cold weather of December 1879. This picture, finished in and dated 1881, was included in the exhibition organized by Durand-Ruel in April 1886 at the American Art Galleries in New York, where it was purchased by A. W. Kingman.

1887

Queen Victoria celebrates the golden jubilee of her reign.

The first Sherlock Holmes mystery story by Arthur Conan Doyle is published: *A Study in Scarlet*.

When Alexander Turney Stewart died in 1877, he left a fortune estimated at $30 million, considered to be at that time the most money ever accumulated by one individual in the United States. He owned a huge department store on Broadway at Ninth Street, and his marble mansion, at the northwest corner of Fifth Avenue and Thirty-fourth Street, was one of the wonders of New York City; its art gallery contained the nation's most extensive and most expensive collection of paintings and statuary.

Stewart, a Scotch-Irish immigrant, had opened a tiny shop in 1823 at 283 Broadway. Thanks to his acute business sense and hard-driving attitude toward the shopgirls he employed, he soon amassed a fortune which, besides the store and mansion, included the Grand Union Hotel in Saratoga and much of what is now Garden City, Long Island, a model community developed by Stewart himself.

After Stewart's death, his body was stolen from the churchyard of St.-Mark's-in-the-Bowery and held until his widow paid $20,000 in ransom. His remains were later reinterred in the Protestant Episcopal Cathedral he had endowed at Garden City.

The auction of his effects, accompanied by both plain and "deluxe" versions of the catalogue, comprised 1,483 lots which took ten sessions to disperse. The total receipts, $575,679, represented something of a disappointment in terms of return on investment, as Stewart had paid *very* high prices *very* recently for *very* big pictures. The largest of all, Adolphe Yvon's *The Genius of America*, measured 22 by 35 feet and did not sell at all. Instead, the painting remained in the Grand Union Hotel at Saratoga until the building was demolished in 1952.

When Stewart's mansion was first built, a writer for *Harper's Weekly* prophesied that "if not swallowed up by an earthquake [the edifice] will stand as long as the city remains, and will ever be pointed to as a monument of individual enterprise, of far-seeing judgment, and of disinterested philanthropy" (August 14, 1869).

Today the mansion, hotel, and store are all gone—only the suburban cathedral on Stewart Avenue and the works of art he owned, which are still seen and admired by many, remind us of this once-famous man.

Hiram Powers. *The Greek Slave*. 1843. Height, including pedestal, 90″. Yale University Art Gallery, New Haven, Connecticut. Olive Louise Dann Fund. Lot 916 in the A. T. Stewart collection auction, managed by the American Art Association and held at Chickering Hall and the American Art Galleries on March 23–25 and 28, 1887.

Hiram Powers's best-known work, one of the most celebrated sculptures of the early nineteenth century, was accepted by the public despite its nudity because it "chastely" portrayed a Christian captive and because it was accepted as an antislavery allegory in pre–Civil War America. (Even so, men and women were required to view *The Greek Slave* separately, not in mixed company, when the sculpture first toured the United States.) Several versions are known. This one, sculpted for Prince Anatole Demidoff, was bought by Stewart for $11,000 in Paris at the sale of the prince's collection in 1870. By 1887 fashion had changed so much that the sculpture brought only $965 at the Stewart sale.

Jean Louis Ernest Meissonier. *Friedland—1807.* 1875. Oil on canvas, 53½ x 95½". The Metropolitan Museum of Art, New York. Gift of Henry Hilton, 1887. Lot 210 in the A. T. Stewart sale, held by the American Art Association on March 23–25 and 28, 1887. It fetched $66,000.

One of Meissonier's most ambitious and admired battle pieces, *Friedland—1807* depicts Napoleon at the zenith of his military career. In the artist's words addressed to his patron, Stewart, "I wanted to paint the love, the adoration of the soldiers for the great Captain in whom they had faith, and for whom they were ready to die." Stewart replied that "the grand painting each day develops such additional beauty and interest that I am constantly deriving new enjoyments from its possession."

Rosa Bonheur. *The Horse Fair.* c. 1853–55. Oil on canvas, 96¼ x 199½". The Metropolitan Museum of Art, New York. Gift of Cornelius Vanderbilt, 1887. Lot 217 in the A. T. Stewart collection sale, managed by the American Art Association and held on the premises and at Chickering Hall on March 23–25 and 28, 1887.

One of the most widely acclaimed and reproduced pictures of the nineteenth century, *The Horse Fair* took Rosa Bonheur (1822–1899) almost a year and a half to paint, during which time she spent whole days at the Paris livestock markets. Owned by the famous London dealer Ernest Gambart, *The Horse Fair* was engraved by Sir Edward Landseer, admired by Queen Victoria, and later owned by William P. Wright of Weehawken, New Jersey, from whom Stewart acquired it.

Purchased for $53,000 at the Stewart sale by Cornelius Vanderbilt and presented immediately to the Metropolitan Museum of Art to be shown at their newly built quarters on Fifth Avenue and Eighty-second Street, it has been a popular favorite ever since.

1888

Benjamin Harrison is elected president of the United States.

Kaiser Wilhelm II accedes to the German throne.

Edward Bellamy's *Looking Backward* is published.

Jules Dupré. *Cattle Watering by a Lake*. Oil on canvas, 18 x 22". Private collection.

This is similar to works by Jules Dupré (1811–1889) included in an auction of "Modern Paintings—Worthy Examples of Foreign and Native Art," held on February 21–23, 1888, at the American Art Galleries.

Most sales in the 1880s were liberally sprinkled with paintings of cattle, sheep, and peasants beneath trees or at the edge of a swamp by Dupré, Charles-Emile Jacque, Constant Troyon, Léon Richet, and other contemporary artists of the French School. These paintings were popular and prices were strong, usually among the highest of the sale.

Acquisition of contemporary art at auction is often thought to be a phenomenon of the post-1960s, whereas, in fact, it has a history going back at least to Victorian times.

---

[1]The asterisk indicates that the price includes a 10 percent buyer's premium. See *Notes and Sources*, page 227.

Pierre-Jules Mène. *Mounted Huntsman of the Reign of Louis XV.* Bronze, length 30". Private collection.

This typical bronze by Pierre-Jules Mène (1810–1879) is similar to examples in the sale of the collection of Henry T. Chapman of Brooklyn, held by the American Art Association at Chickering Hall on April 13–14 and 16, 1888.

Mène, one of the lesser-known *animalier* sculptors of the late nineteenth century, has long enjoyed a following among American collectors. The Chapman collection contained many such bronzes.

The cast illustrated here brought $16,500* in October 1982 at Sotheby Parke Bernet, New York.[1]

Rogier van der Weyden. *Saint Luke Painting the Virgin*. c. 1435. Oil on panel, 54¼ x 43¾″. Museum of Fine Arts, Boston, Massachusetts. Gift of Mr. and Mrs. Henry Lee Higginson. Lot 67 in the auction of Old Masters belonging to His Highness Don Pedro de Borbón, Duque de Durcal, managed by the American Art Association and held at Chickering Hall on April 10–11, 1889. The painting had been in the Spanish royal collection since the 1830s.

Tradition holds the figure of Saint Luke to be a self-portrait by van der Weyden and the picture to be his "presentation piece" required for admission to the painters' guild of Brussels, in about 1435.

Henry Lee Higginson (1834–1919), who gave the painting to the Museum of Fine Arts, was a Brahmin financier and founder of the Boston Symphony. *Saint Luke* was the first major Flemish painting to enter an American public collection, fittingly the gift of a generous benefactor whose favorite motto, taken from the Duke of Devonshire's epitaph, was:

> *What I gave, I have*
> *What I shared, I had*
> *What I kept, I lost.*

1889/1890

Montana, Washington, and North and South Dakota are admitted to the Union.

Vincent van Gogh paints *Starry Night*.

Henrick Ibsen writes *Hedda Gabler*.

Antoine Louis Barye. *Theseus and the Minotaur.* c. 1848. Bronze, height 17¾". The Brooklyn Museum, New York. Friends of the Museum, Special Subscription.

This may be the bronze that was exhibited at the American Art Galleries in 1889–90, when the Barye Monument Association (whose members included collectors Cyrus J. Lawrence, William T. Walters, and Henry G. Marquand) sponsored a show of Barye bronzes "for the purpose of raising funds for the erection of a monument in Paris" to his memory.

Admission was fifty cents, and since this exhibition coincided with the first public showing in America of *The Angelus,* attendance was high and success was assured.

Barye (1795–1875) was enormously popular among wealthy American collectors of the day. As Henry James remarked, "To have on one's mantelshelf or one's library table one of [his] business-like little lions diving into the entrails of a jackal, or one of his consummate leopards licking his fangs over a lacerated kid, has long been considered the mark, I will not say of a refined, but at least of an enterprising taste." W. W. Corcoran left his collection of Barye bronzes to the museum in Washington, D.C., that bears his name. This Brooklyn Museum example was acquired in 1910 at the auction of the collection of Cyrus J. Lawrence, who was a lender to the 1889–90 show.

The Barye Monument was erected in Paris in 1894, at the east end of the Ile St.-Louis, in a small garden overlooking the Seine.

Jean-François Millet. *The Angelus*. c. 1858–59. Oil on canvas, 21⅝ x 26⅜″. Musée du Louvre, Paris. Alfred Chauchard Bequest, 1906.

The worldwide popularity—notoriety, in fact—of Millet's *The Angelus* owes much to its purchase, exhibition, and sale by the American Art Association in 1889–90.

In the years between 1858–59, when *The Angelus* was painted, and 1889, when it appeared in the M. E. Secrétan auction in Paris, the picture had changed hands half-a-dozen times. It had also risen in value, reflecting the painter's growing reputation, from 1,800 francs to what was the highest price paid for any picture at an auction in the nineteenth century: 553,000 francs (about $110,000). The successful

bidder was a representative of the French government. James Sutton, representing the American Art Association, was underbidder, however, and when the French refused to allocate the necessary funds, *The Angelus* was sold to Sutton, who triumphantly brought it to America, where in a patriotic gesture Customs dropped the usual 30-percent duty on this celebrated picture.

In mid-November, a special exhibition opened at the American Art Galleries. According to the *New York Times*, "The Angelus is naturally the great point of attraction. It hangs at the northern end of the topmost gallery against a drapery of dark crimson plush fit for the setting of a throne, and is railed away from

the too curious by brass posts and crimson ropes."

Thanks to the crowds, newspaper articles, and reproductions in many mediums, *The Angelus* became an image as well known to Americans as the *Mona Lisa* or *The Last Supper*.

Attempts were made to buy the picture for an American museum, but when nothing materialized, the American Art Association sold *The Angelus* to Alfred Chauchard, director of the Magasins du Louvre, who bequeathed the work to the Musée du Louvre. There it hangs today, seen by thousands of tourists who have no idea that it once hung in 1890 "against a drapery of dark crimson" in a gallery on East Twenty-third Street, in New York City.

1891

Jean Louis Ernest Meissonier. *Playing at Bowls in the Fosse at Antibes.* 1885. Oil on panel, 17½ x 30¼". Arnot Art Museum, Elmira, New York. Arnot Bequest, 1910. Lot 190 in the second George I. Seney auction, American Art Galleries, February 11–13, 1891. The price was $15,000.

Best known for his meticulously painted battlepieces and depictions of everyday life in the seventeenth century, Meissonier occasionally painted landscapes with small figures, as in this scene near the old fortifications at Antibes on the Riviera.

It is difficult for us today to share the excitement that must have been felt by collectors of "acceptable" contemporary painting in the late nineteenth century. Artists who had found the right formula and who showed at the annual Salons in Paris were almost always assured of sales and success—especially if their creations found favor with the hordes of newly rich Americans who flocked to the Continent for education, culture, and excitement.

Eugène Isabey (1803–1886) was equally adept at seascapes, stormy coastal landscapes, historical paintings, and genre scenes of bygone days. He was also an official painter to King Louis Philippe. Two slightly later painters even more prolific than Isabey, whom he influenced, were equally popular with American collectors of the Gilded Age: Narcisse-Virgile Diaz de la Peña and Adolph Joseph Thomas Monticelli.

J.L.E. Meissonier (1815–1891) was one of the most successful and wealthy painters of all time. Although he began as a poor man (charging 5 francs for a picture), he worked hard (up to thirteen hours a day) and by 1862 was said to be making 150,000 francs annually. After his death, a sale of the contents of his studio was held in Paris. Almost a thousand lots were listed in a huge and impressive catalogue. Meissonier, after all, was the darling of the Establishment, whose members, in this era of violent political and financial turmoil, labor unrest, anarchists, and populists, preferred their artists to be spokesmen for the prevailing order. Disciplined soldiers, happy peasants, bucolic farm scenes, and pious portraits were most in demand. Small wonder that Horace Vernet's *Socialism and Cholera* was described in the catalogue in such detail when it appeared in the J. H. Stebbins sale at the American Art Association just a few years earlier:

> It is a scene of horror, under a sky of dread. Upon the guillotine a victim is bound to the fatal plank. Perched upon him as on a throne, Death and the Plague hold rule over a great field of carnage. Corpses are everywhere . . . in the horror-haunted gloom. They are the fruits of socialism; they typify socialism itself, which, as the artist holds, can only end in destruction, carnage, annihilation, and a restoration of the old and natural social order.

The natural social order according to Isabey and Meissonier was far more comforting to collectors of the day.

Louis Gabriel Eugène Isabey. *Saint Hubert's Day.* Oil on cradled panel, 67 x 49″. Private collection. Lot 307 in the "Catalogue of Mr. George I. Seney's Important Collection of Modern Paintings," published for the second Seney auction, American Art Galleries, February 11–13, 1891. It brought $4,000.

Isabey specialized in genre scenes depicting aristocratic life in earlier times. Shown here is the annual ceremony of the blessing of the hounds on November 3, the feast day of Saint Hubert, patron of huntsmen. Geraldine Rockefeller Dodge, who later owned the picture, was celebrated for her love of animals. Her shelter for dogs in Madison, New Jersey, was called St. Hubert's - Giralda. On May 14, 1976, her painting was sold at Sotheby Parke Bernet in New York, lot 48, for $18,000.

1892

Grover Cleveland is elected president of the United States.

William Gladstone is reelected prime minister of Great Britain.

Dr. Charles Parkhurst launches his civic reform movement to clean up vice and crime in New York City.

Pair of urns. Japanese, Meiji period (late nineteenth century). Cloisonné enamel, height 38 inches.

These urns are similar to many elaborate pieces sold in the auction of April 7–8, 1892, at the American Art Association's dispersal of their own holdings at Chickering Hall. R. Austin Robertson, an associate of James Sutton's since the 1880s, had represented the Association in China and Japan, buying objects for sale in New York either at retail or at auction.

Vast quantities of cloisonné enamels, colorful porcelains, elaborately carved hardstones, and intricately woven textiles were imported into the United States during the last decade of the nineteenth century and the first decade of the twentieth century, before large-scale excavations and intensive scholarship brought about a well-founded appreciation of the ancient arts of the Orient. These vases, decorated with red and white poppies on a pale blue ground, typical of much Japanese art auctioned in the 1890s, might have fetched a few hundred dollars at that time. In July 1980, when these urns were sold at Sotheby Parke Bernet, New York, they brought $9,900*.

Edward Lamson Henry. *The Old Westover Mansion*. 1869. Oil on panel, 11¼ x 14⅝". Corcoran Gallery of Art, Washington, D.C. Gift of the American Art Association, 1900. Lot 102 in the auction sale held by the American Art Association on the occasion of R. Austin Robertson's withdrawal from the Association, at Chickering Hall on April 7–8, 1892. The price was $150.

Perhaps the sale of this picture was not consummated or perhaps the Association bought it themselves. In any case, the painting was donated to the Corcoran Gallery eight years later.

Edward Lamson Henry (1841–1919) is renowned for his painstakingly faithful depictions of America's Colonial past. His popularity rose during the second half of the nineteenth century with the gradual rediscovery and reappreciation of the Colonial and early Federal way of life.

Westover, on the James River in Virginia, was built in the 1730s by William Byrd II, a wealthy planter who had a library of 3,600 volumes. The plantation was occupied by General Grant in 1864, during the Civil War, at which time Henry made the sketches for this painting.

1893

Frederic Remington (1861–1909) was one of America's best-known illustrators during the 1880s and 1890s, but as late as 1893 his reputation as a painter (not just an illustrator) of the American West was not as yet established. Hoping to rectify this situation by showing and selling some of his pictures in New York, Remington arranged to have an exhibition and auction at the American Art Association. Ninety-seven drawings, watercolors, and paintings were included, the highlights being *A Lull in the Fight* (which Remington had shown at the International Exposition in Paris in 1889) and *The Last Stand,* his depiction of Custer at the Little Big Horn.

Despite an enthusiastic and well-attended pre-sale exhibition, Remington was justifiably disappointed in the results of the auction. One of the journalists who covered the event commented, "Mr. Remington's preeminence as an artist of the Far West was readily recognized in the prices paid for his illustrations, while some of his paintings failed to reach the expected figure." *The Last Stand* did not sell, and Remington netted only about $7,000 in all for his efforts.

'Turn Him Loose!'—*Breaking a Bronco* (as it was catalogued in the 1893 sale) was purchased by Joseph Byfield of Chicago for $170, and the canvas later passed into the collection of Mr. and Mrs. Kay Kimbell of Fort Worth, Texas. It was sold by the Kimbell Art Foundation at Sotheby Parke Bernet in New York (lot 14) on October 16, 1974, for $175,000.

Disappointed but not defeated, Remington held another exhibition and auction at the Association galleries in 1895. In this sale he concentrated on the black-and-white sketches and paintings that had been done as magazine illustrations. Again the results were unspectacular, but in that same year Remington produced his first and best-known bronze, *The Bronco-Buster.* Fame as a sculptor and painter was not far away.

Frederic Remington, *The Bronco-Buster.* Bronze, height 23". Signed and numbered N 156. Cast by the Roman Bronze Works, New York.

This example of Remington's first and most popular sculpture was sold at Sotheby Parke Bernet in October 1977 for $33,000. It is estimated that some 250 examples of the piece were cast by the Roman Bronze Works, in addition to the first 40 or so cast by the Henry Bonnard Bronze Company between 1895 and 1898.

Frederic Remington, *'Turn Him Loose, Bill.'* Oil on canvas, mounted on masonite, 25 x 33". Private collection. As *'Turn Him Loose!'*—*Breaking a Bronco,* lot 53 in the artist's auction sale, American Art Galleries, January 13, 1893. It fetched $170.

1894

Labor unrest is widespread in the United States; "Coxey's Army" invades Washington and bloody strikes occur.

In France, Alfred Dreyfus is sentenced to imprisonment on Devil's Island.

James Tissot. *Without Dowry.* c. 1883–85. Oil on canvas, 57⅞ x 41⅜". Collection of Mr. and Mrs. Joseph M. Tanenbaum, Toronto, Ontario. Lot 210 in the George I. Seney estate sale, Chickering Hall and the American Art Galleries, February 7–10, 1894. The picture brought $510.

James Tissot (1836–1902), born in Nantes and educated in Paris, left the capital after the fall of the Commune in 1871 and moved to London, where he enjoyed some success as a painter. He returned to Paris in 1882. In order to reestablish his reputation in France, Tissot began a series of fifteen large paintings collectively entitled *La Femme à Paris,* celebrating the multifaceted Parisian woman in her many manifestations: in politics, in fashion, as circus performer, as artist's wife, and so forth.

When *Without Dowry,* one of the works from this series, was exhibited in London at Arthur Tooth & Sons gallery in 1886, the catalogue described the painting in detail, noting, "It is Versailles, under the trees . . . the summer is over, the winter is coming, to her as to the world. And so another year has gone, and she is twelve months nearer old maidenhood than she was a year ago."

The cataloguer of the American Art Association's third and final George I. Seney collection sale completely missed the point: he described the picture, titled *A Parisian Afternoon,* as a scene in the Tuileries Gardens, with a lady reading the paper as her daughter crochets and flirts with soldiers. The canvas sold for far less than Ludwig Knaus's *Coffee Hour* (the hit of the sale at $8,200).

Tissot, like so many artists of the "other nineteenth century"—that of the Salon painters and other conservative non-Impressionists—has enjoyed a tremendous resurgence of interest during the 1970s and 1980s.

1895

Oscar Wilde's *The Importance of Being Earnest* and Stephen Crane's *The Red Badge of Courage* are published.

Guglielmo Marconi invents the wireless telegraph.

Claude Monet. *Two Vases of Chrysanthemums.* 1888. Oil on canvas, 28½ x 36". Private collection. Lot 86 in the James F. Sutton sale, Chickering Hall, April 25–27 and 29–30, 1895. It sold for $675.

"Catalogue of the Extremely Valuable and Highly Artistic Property Belonging to the American Art Association, New York, acquired by them since the fall of 1892, and to be sold on account of Mr. James F. Sutton withdrawing as an active member of the Association." So read the title of the auction that marked the end of the Sutton era at the Association. Works by Berthe Morisot, Paul Signac, Odilon Redon, Alfred Sisley, and Armand Guillaumin were included beside the usual array of more conventional works and a group "picked by Mr. Bing [the famous Paris art dealer and promoter of Art Nouveau] as being representative of rising young French artists." The man who had brought the Impressionists to New York in 1886 was now retiring and selling off the works he had accumulated for the Association's inventory.

With this sale of almost six-hundred lots of paintings, the old, retailing/dealing tradition of the American Art Association came to an end as Thomas E. Kirby, auctioneer *par excellence,* took over complete control of the company he had helped to organize a dozen years previously.

1896

William McKinley is elected president of the United States on the Republican ticket, defeating William Jennings Bryan, the "Free-silver Democrat."

Henri de Toulouse-Lautrec's series of lithographs *Elles* is published.

Auctions of carpets, tapestries, and Japanese art, as well as a group of "curios" consigned by William Merritt Chase, enlivened the sales held by the American Art Association in 1896. The high point of the season for conservative collectors was no doubt the auction of "Masterpieces by Famous Painters and an Extraordinary Carved Ivory Casket" from the collection of William Schaus. Two of the pictures from this sale found their way to the Metropolitan Museum of Art: Rousseau's *The Edge of the Woods at Mont-Girard* and Daubigny's *River Landscape with Storks*.

Nowadays, when asked to describe paintings by a French artist named Rousseau most people mention sleeping gypsies and exotic jungles, so strong has been the impact of the Douanier on modern sensibilities. But in 1896 Henri Rousseau, called "Douanier," had only recently retired from his job as a customs collector in order to devote his energies to painting, and Pierre-Etienne-Théodore Rousseau (1812–1867) was still one of the most admired—and expensive—of the Barbizon School painters. He was also the acknowledged leader of that group, which included Millet, Diaz, Dupré, Troyon, and Daubigny (Corot is correctly considered the forerunner and "godfather" rather than a member of the school).

The Edge of the Woods, one of Rousseau's most significant works, done just before he first achieved public recognition at the Paris World's Fair in 1855, shows the influence of earlier Dutch and English painters whose pure landscapes so shocked French viewers. It is interesting to note that this painting was an early environmentalist protest statement: Rousseau had tried to stop a forest-clearing project near Fontainebleau and here he recorded for posterity the trees that would soon be uprooted by the government.

Charles-François Daubigny (1817–1878) first came into his own as a painter when he joined the Barbizon group in the 1840s. In 1860 he settled at Auvers, a village that was his home for the rest of his life, although he traveled extensively in his floating studio on rivers throughout France.

A River Landscape with Storks was sold twice at the American Art Association: once in 1896, and again on January 8–9, 1903, as lot 69 in Mrs. S. D. Warren's sale. On the latter occasion it was described as "a harmony of cool, juicy greens... exquisitely suggestive of the stillness and refreshment of deepening twilight... a charming subject in Daubigny's most intimate manner." This time the price was $9,300.

Opposite above: Théodore Rousseau. *The Edge of the Woods at Mont-Girard.* 1854. Oil on wood panel, 31½ x 48″. The Metropolitan Museum of Art, New York. Wolfe Fund, 1896. Catherine Lorillard Wolfe Collection. Lot 16, William Schaus collection sale, American Art Association, February 28, 1896. The purchase price was $25,200.

Opposite below: Charles-François Daubigny. *A River Landscape with Storks.* 1864. Oil on wood panel, 9½ x 17⅝″. The Metropolitan Museum of Art, New York. Bequest of Benjamin Altman, 1913. Lot 7, William Schaus auction, American Art Association, February 28, 1896. The picture sold for $4,200.

1897

One of the Association's big sales of 1897 was a three-evening auction comprised almost entirely of works by Jacob Maris (1837–1899), Anton Mauve (1838–1888), Jozef Israels (1824–1911), and other painters of The Hague School, the Dutch counterpart of the Barbizon School in France, whose chief interest was in the simple lives of Dutch peasant-farmers.

Hendrik Weissenbruch, Hendrik Mesdag, and others were also represented—artists whose work can usually be seen today only in auction galleries and a few Dutch museums. Prices at the sale were generally in the low-to-mid-hundreds of dollars, though Jozef Israels's large *Grace before Meals* sold for $3,100 in 1892, an indication of his popularity at that time.

Vincent van Gogh, related to Anton Mauve by marriage, was profoundly influenced by him and his colleagues. While working at The Hague in 1870–73, and again in 1881, when he actually painted with Mauve, van Gogh absorbed many of the tenets of The Hague School, a now almost forgotten group of artists.

Jozef Israels. *The Bargeman*. Oil on canvas, 22½ x 47½". Private collection.

This painting is typical of the works by Israels sold at the American Art Association's auction of the collection of the Holland Art Galleries at Chickering Hall on February 24–26, 1897. *The Bargeman* was sold in October 1981 at Sotheby Parke Bernet, New York, for $11,000*.

Anton Mauve. *Homeward Bound*. Oil on canvas, 27¼ x 47½". Private collection.

Mauve was represented in the Holland Art Galleries sale at Chickering Hall on February 24–26, 1897, though this canvas, owned at one time by William Randolph Hearst, was not among them. It might have fetched $500 then; in 1934 it was sold at the American Art Association–Anderson Galleries for $1,300; in 1979, at Sotheby Parke Bernet, New York, it realized $41,800*.

1898

Theodore Robinson. *On the Canal*. 1893. Oil on canvas, 18 x 22″. Private collection. Lot 82 in the Theodore Robinson sale held on March 24, 1898, at the American Art Galleries was bought by Samuel T. Shaw for $300.

In 1926, when the Samuel T. Shaw collection was auctioned at the American Art Association, *On the Canal* brought $1,525, and in December 1983, it was included in an auction of American paintings at Sotheby Parke Bernet, New York. The price this time was $209,000*.

The picture was painted on the Delaware and Hudson Canal, at Port Ben (or Port Benjamin), near Ellenville, in Ulster County, New York.

Theodore Robinson (1852–1896) is generally considered the first and the finest of the American Impressionists. He visited France initially in 1876 and in 1887 painted at Giverny, where he came under the influence of Monet. Fame and fortune eluded him, however, and on March 30, 1896, Robinson died suddenly in New York City, poor and alone; fellow artists paid his funeral expenses.

Two years later an auction of ninety-four works left unsold at the time of Robinson's death was held at the American Art Association. Unappreciated during his lifetime, Robinson's paintings fared badly in the sale. The highest price commanded was $300, for *On the Canal,* and most of the pictures went for $50 or less. Yet the list of buyers' names is an impressive one: among the prominent collectors who bid successfully were architect Stanford White, music publisher G. Schirmer, merchant George A. Hearn, and Brooklyn financier G. B. Pratt.

Girl Sewing (as *The Layette* was then described) is mentioned in the artist's diaries twice: first, in an entry of October 1892, where Robinson records that he worked at Giverny, "with Yvonne on large *Layette*"; later, in 1894, after seeing the picture in a show at the Pennsylvania Academy of the Fine Arts, he notes, "My *Layette* not *entirely* bad."

At the American Art Association auction, *The Layette* was sold for $200 to George A. Hearn. When Hearn's noted collection was sold at the American Art Association in 1918, *The Layette* (still called *Girl Sewing*) was bought by the Corcoran Gallery for $5,000.

Theodore Robinson. *The Layette*. 1892. Oil on canvas, 58⅛ x 36¼". Corcoran Gallery of Art, Washington, D.C. Museum Purchase. As *Girl Sewing*, lot 56 in the artist's estate sale held on March 24, 1898, at the American Art Galleries. The price: $200.

1899

Treaty of Paris ending Spanish-American War is ratified by the United States Congress.

Philosopher-educator John Dewey writes his revolutionary *The School and Society.*

The story of collecting in America during the second half of the nineteenth century is inextricably linked with the name of Thomas Benedict Clarke—businessman, clubman, collector, dealer, patron, connoisseur, and promoter.

Born in 1848, Clarke made a fortune in the collar-and-cuffs manufacturing business and began to acquire contemporary American art in the 1870s, when he bought many works by Inness and Homer. In later life he took up Chinese ceramics, historical portraits, English furniture, and Americana. He remained a force in various fields of collecting until his death in 1930.

As early as 1884, Clarke had exhibited his private collection at the American Art Association. At that time he already owned a painting by Anschutz called *Ironworkers' Noontime,* and the critics were enthusiastic in their praise of it. Thomas P. Anschutz (1851–1912), a pupil of Thomas Eakins, was a respected teacher at the Pennsylvania Academy of the Fine Arts, counting among his pupils Charles Sheeler and John Marin. Perhaps its subject matter, reminding visitors to the galleries of the labor strife so common in American industry at the time, was responsible for the low price commanded by the powerful work at the Clarke sale.

A Garden (as it was then catalogued) by Thomas W. Dewing (1851–1938) fared somewhat better, for Charles Lang Freer of Detroit paid $375 for it. Freer eventually owned a large number of Dewing's works, many of which can still be seen in the museum at Washington, D.C., to which he bequeathed his name, his fortune, and his collections. *The Garden,* however, he gave to his friend Stanford White, a patron of Dewing who also designed frames for him, and it was eventually left to the Museum of Fine Arts in Boston by George H. Webster, who had bought it at the Stanford White auction in 1905.

The Garden is one of Dewing's first paintings in the Aesthetic manner; it shows the influence of Sir Lawrence Alma-Tadema in the placement of the figures.

Thomas B. Clarke had always been a staunch promoter of George Inness. There were no fewer than thirty-nine Innesses in the auction, and the artist's *Grey, Lowering Day* brought the highest price of the sale, $10,150. But it was Winslow Homer (1836–1910) who was to benefit most from his patron's auction. Thirty-one works by the Maine artist were sold on those winter evenings in 1899. *The Life Line* brought $4,500, and *Eight Bells* fetched $4,700—the highest prices in the Clarke sale for a work by a living artist. *Eight Bells,* one of Homer's greatest and best-known paintings, profoundly manifests the artist's respect for the sea and the men whose lives were intimately involved with it.

When Homer heard the news, he wrote to Clarke, saying, "I owe it to you to express to you my sincere thanks for the great benefit that I have received from your encouragement of my work and to congratulate you...only think of my being *alive* with a reputation (that you have made for me)." And indeed, Clarke had done much for Homer, arranging shows for him at the Century Association and elsewhere, praising Homer to his wide circle of acquaintances, and in general making the artist's name one to be reckoned with in New York as well as in Boston, where his dealers, Doll & Richards, were located.

The Thomas B. Clarke sale was a benchmark in the history of American collecting, and Clarke's influence is still felt, though, sadly, little recognized.

Thomas Wilmer Dewing. *The Garden* (or *Autumn*). 1883. Oil on canvas, 16 x 40". Museum of Fine Arts, Boston, Massachusetts. Bequest of George H. Webster. Lot 246 in the American Art Association's Thomas B. Clarke sale, Chickering Hall, February 14–17, 1899. The price was $375.

Opposite: Thomas Pollock Anschutz. *Ironworkers—Noontime.* c. 1880–82. Oil on canvas, 17 x 24". The Fine Arts Museums of San Francisco, M. H. de Young Memorial Museum. Gift of Mr. and Mrs. John D. Rockefeller III. Lot 56 in the Thomas B. Clarke collection sale, Chickering Hall, February 14–17, 1899. It brought $150.

On October 18, 1972, as *Steelworkers' Noontime,* the picture was sold at Sotheby Parke Bernet, New York, in the Dr. and Mrs. Irving F. Burton collection auction, lot 14, for $250,000.

Winslow Homer. *Eight Bells*. 1886. Oil on canvas, 24 x 30″. Addison Gallery of American Art, Phillips Academy, Andover, Massachusetts. Lot 370 in the American Art Association's Thomas B. Clarke sale at Chickering Hall, February 14–17, 1899, fetched $4,700.

1900

Boxers, a Chinese secret society, seize control of Beijing.

The Wonderful Wizard of Oz by L. F. Baum is published.

Ralph Albert Blakelock. *The Three Trees.* c. 1885. Oil on canvas, 22 x 30″. Hirshhorn Museum and Sculpture Garden, Smithsonian Institution, Washington, D.C. Probably lot 110 in the sale of the collection of William T. Evans, held by the American Art Association at Chickering Hall on January 31 and February 1–2, 1900. The price was $250.

Ralph Blakelock (1847–1919) was a gifted but eccentric American artist whose works were generally ignored before 1900, by which time he had been confined to an insane asylum, where he spent most of the rest of his life.

He painted landscapes (*The Three Trees* epitomizes Blakelock's romantic treatment of unspoiled nature), Indian encampments, and views of still wooded areas of New York City. After about 1905, prices for his works began to appreciate, but an avalanche of crude fakes engulfed the market during the early years of this century, hurting his reputation among educated collectors. In some respects the Blakelock market has never truly recovered from the onslaught of imitations.

1901

Theodore Roosevelt becomes president of the United States after William McKinley is assassinated.

Queen Victoria dies and is succeeded on the British throne by her son Edward VII.

Anonymous photographer. *View of the Piazzetta, Venice.* c. 1895. Lot 264 in the sale of the collection of Charles E. West, held by John Anderson, Jr., at his gallery at 34 West Thirtieth Street on May 27, 1901.

In 1900 John Anderson, Jr., founded what would become the Anderson Auction Company, a rival of the American Art Association. His firm specialized in sales of books and prints, although occasional art auctions were also held. It was later renamed Anderson Galleries, and in 1929 it merged with the American Art Association. Travel albums of photographic views were included in Anderson's massive sale of the collection of Professor West of Brooklyn. Lot 264 was listed as "Venice, St. Mark's Square. A tinted photograph, neatly framed."

The West sales continued through the entire year, beginning with books in May, prints and books in June, and more prints and books in October.

Meanwhile, the American Art Galleries offered a mixed sale from the professor's collection in March. Thirteen hundred eighty-five lots included books on art, contemporary prints, a large group of drawings by William Blake, and, of course, photographs, mostly collected in albums and sold as adjuncts to prints.

Auctions composed entirely of photographica and photographs were not held until 1967 at Parke-Bernet Galleries but they have since become a staple of the auction market.

1902

First of Frank Lloyd Wright's "prairie houses" is built in Illinois.

Edouard Manet. *The Smoker.* 1866. Oil on canvas, 39½ x 32¼". The Minneapolis Institute of Arts. Gift of Mr. and Mrs. Bruce B. Dayton, 1968. Lot 18 in the sale of the collection of E. F. Milliken, held under the management of the American Art Association, at Mendelssohn Hall, Broadway and Fortieth Street, on February 14, 1902. It was sold to Durand-Ruel for $3,100 and later was in the collection of Mrs. Harry Payne Whitney. Her daughter, Mrs. G. McCullough Miller, sold the painting at auction at Sotheby Parke-Bernet, New York, on October 14, 1965, lot 114, for $450,000.

In this year the American Art Association held auctions of everything from Japanese prints and rare textiles to Oriental carvings, but two important sales of paintings nevertheless stood out.

The E. F. Milliken auction included several fine paintings by the Impressionists; works by some of their like-minded American contemporaries such as William Merritt Chase, Homer D. Martin, and J. Alden Weir; plus the inevitable Corots, Millets, and Daubignys. Perhaps the most unusual lot was a portrait said to be of Giorgio Cornaro and ascribed to Titian.

Theron J. Blakeslee, who gave his name to numerous sales at the American Art Association (and elsewhere) during the early part of the century, was a dealer who apparently specialized in what the art trade called "painted ladies"—heavily varnished portraits of beautiful women, optimistically attributed to the biggest names in the history of art. Whenever Blakeslee got into financial difficulty, which was quite often, he would consign another group of pictures until, after a particularly bad period during which he was stuck with a *Blue Boy* claimed by him to be the original Gainsborough canvas, he committed suicide.

All that was far in the future, however, and the 1902 group was on the whole a rather impressive one. Even so, *The Trellis,* catalogued as *Jeune Femme Cueillant des Fleurs,* did not bring a very high price in spite of its important size and its attractive subject matter. Courbet's paintings were not unusual items at American Art Association auctions: three had been sold in 1886 and one fetched $6,200 less than a year after Mr. Blakeslee's "clearance sale." The French firm Durand-Ruel was, in 1902, the fortunate buyer of *The Trellis.*

Gustave Courbet. *The Trellis.* c. 1862. Oil on canvas, 43¼ x 53¼". The Toledo Museum of Art, Toledo, Ohio. Gift of Edward Drummond Libbey. As *Jeune Femme Cueillant des Fleurs,* lot 50 in the sale of the T. J. Blakeslee collection, held at Mendelssohn Hall under the management of the American Art Association on April 10–11, 1902. The selling price was $550.

1903

With the help of the United States, Panama declares its independence from Colombia, a preliminary to the building of the Panama Canal.

Theodore Roosevelt's *Outdoor Pastimes of an American Hunter* spurs interest in nature, the outdoor life, and the environment.

Paul Gauguin dies in Tahiti.

The sale of the collection of Barbizon paintings belonging to the pioneer Boston collector Mrs. S. D. Warren got the year off to a good start on January 8, and two weeks later one of the most illustrious auctions ever held in New York took place when the Henry G. Marquand collection was sold on January 23 at Mendelssohn Hall and on January 24–31 at the American Art Galleries on Madison Square.

Henry Gurdon Marquand (1819–1902) was a well-known New York railroad magnate, financier, philanthropist, and art patron, who was also one of the original organizers of the Metropolitan Museum of Art, serving as its second president from 1889 to 1902. His mansion at Madison Avenue and Sixty-eighth Street, designed by architect Richard Morris Hunt, was filled with art treasures of every description: paintings by the leading contemporary artists as well as Old Masters of the English School, Chinese porcelains, Japanese daggers and carved toggles *(netsukes),* English silver and porcelain, ancient glass, Greek vases, Limoges enamels, antique intaglios, Persian pottery, armor, embroideries, textiles, carpets, tapestries, engravings, books, and furniture. Russell Sturgis, an eminent architectural critic of the time, in his introduction to the sale catalogue appropriately compared Marquand to an Italian Renaissance prince and related how the late owner would "chase the elusive thing with more energy than another, [and] therefore, he secured the prize...[the rooms of his house] were marvels of splendid variety, differing in nothing from the palace interiors which we dream of existing in the great times of creative art." Here he must have been referring to the music salon, whose furnishings, including a piano, wallpaper, upholstery, and draperies, were specially designed for Marquand by Sir Lawrence Alma-Tadema in the antique taste.

As if to silence those who may have felt that 2,154 catalogued lots of such splendor were a bit much for any one person to own, Sturgis concluded his essay by declaring, "It was not really confusion; it was profusion. The splendor of one rich work of art need never do harm to the tranquil sweetness of another. He must be a far less sagacious student of art than was the owner of these treasures, if it be ever found in his beloved rooms that there is too much of anything, no matter how much there may be."

Grecian music room in the Henry G. Marquand house, Sixty-eighth Street and Madison Avenue.

Millefleurs prayer rug. Indian, Mughal period (late seventeenth century). Silk, 65 x 44". Private collection, Mannheim, Germany. Lot 1285 in the H. G. Marquand sale held on January 31, 1903, listed in the American Art Association's catalogue as "Old Persian," was bought by the famous dealer Vitall Benguiat for $7,000.

In 1925 it brought $8,800 at an American Art Association auction; in 1969 the Kevorkian Foundation sold it at Sotheby's, London, for £2,000; and in 1976 the present owner acquired it at a Sotheby's, London, sale for £17,000.

Luca della Robbia. *Madonna in a Niche.* c. 1450. Enameled terra-cotta, 19 x 15¼". The Metropolitan Museum of Art. Bequest of Susan Dwight Bliss, 1966. Lot 1198 in the H. G. Marquand sale at the American Art Association, January 24–31, 1903, fetched $8,600.

The plaque, formerly in the collection of Emile Gavet, Paris, had been extensively studied and published by the leading scholars of the day, including Allan Marquand, Henry Marquand's son, of the art history department at Princeton University, who wrote authoritative monographs on the della Robbia family of sculptors.

Sir Lawrence Alma-Tadema. *A Reading From Homer.* 1885. Oil on canvas, 36 x 72". Philadelphia Museum of Art. Lot 88 in the American Art Association's H. G. Marquand sale at Mendelssohn Hall on January 23, 1903, brought $30,300—the highest price for a single object in the entire Marquand auction. The lengthy catalogue description read in part, "The spirit of the old Greek life...revived in this picture with the fullness of learning and the reasonableness of suggestion that render the work of Alma-Tadema unique."

Concert grand piano, designed by Sir Lawrence Alma-Tadema, the works by Steinway, the painted panel by Sir Edward John Poynter. c. 1886. Sandalwood and ebony inlaid with cedar, ivory, coral, and mother-of-pearl. Private collection, New York. This instrument, together with a pair of matching stools, were lots 1363 and 1365 in the H. G. Marquand sale held at the American Art Galleries on January 31, 1903. The piano brought $8,000, the stools $1,050—all going to William Barbour of New York. They were later displayed in the lobby of the Martin Beck Theater, New York, and sold at an auction at PB Eighty-Four, Sotheby Parke Bernet's salesroom at 171 East Eighty-fourth Street, on May 26, 1980, for $429,000*.

Thomas Cole. *The Titan's Goblet*. c. 1833. Oil on canvas, 19⅜ x 16⅛″. The Metropolitan Museum of Art. Gift of Samuel P. Avery, Jr., 1904. Lot 407 in the sale of the collection of John M. Falconer of Brooklyn at the Anderson Auction Company on April 28–29, 1904, fetched $150.

Thomas Cole (1801–1848) came to America as a youth from his native England. He was one of the founders and leaders of the Hudson River School, America's first school of painting, influenced by the romantic and transcendental philosophies of the early nineteenth century.

Said to have been painted for the artist's chief patron, Luman Reed, *The Titan's Goblet* may allude to the Norse legend of Yggdrasil, tree of the world. It dates from the period when Cole was planning his *Course of Empire* series, now in the New-York Historical Society.

Falconer, who knew Cole, published a pamphlet in 1886 describing *The Titan's Goblet* as "a grand picture of symbolic art. What is this vast goblet but the little world of man . . . a cosmos. . . . The goblet is the microcosm, man. The earth, upon which it rests, which stretches beyond, around and beneath it, is the vast[ness] of nature. Man has absorbed this nature. . . . The outer world is reproduced and present in him."

Staffordshire Historical Blue pottery platter showing Mendenhall Ferry (Joseph Stubbs Manufactory). c. 1825. Length 16¾". Private collection.

This platter is similar to one that brought $30 as lot 602 in the sale of "antique furniture, 'Historical Blue China,' and other objects of American interest, the property of John Jay Gilbert, Baltimore." The auction was held at the American Art Galleries on November 21–23, 1904.

This was an early sale of what would today be called Americana, that is, furniture and decorative or useful accessories made in what are now the eastern United States, or made abroad but used in America during the eighteenth and nineteenth centuries. So-called Historical Blue china was transfer-printed dinnerware made at many factories in Staffordshire, England, primarily for export to the United States. The decoration of this pottery consisted generally of American or English scenes copied from prints. The most popular were ultrapatriotic in nature—befitting a new nation that had only recently concluded its *second* war with Great Britain. Vast quantities of this Staffordshire blue-and-white dinnerware were exported to the United States.

The piece illustrated here brought $412.50* at a Sotheby Parke Bernet sale in New York in 1981.

1905

Portsmouth, New Hampshire, Peace Conference concludes the Russo-Japanese War.

Derogatory term *fauves* ("wild beasts") is first applied to Matisse, Derain, and other avant-garde artists exhibiting at the Paris Salon.

Franz Lehar composes his operetta *The Merry Widow*.

A vogue for works of art reflecting decorative styles and subjects of the Near East sprang up in Europe after Napoleon's occupation of Egypt between 1798 and 1801. Later French incursions into North Africa opened up a whole new world of possibilities for architects, artists, craftsmen, and collectors.

Just as *chinoiserie* and *japonnerie* had been all the rage during the eighteenth century, so the newly opened Moslem territories furnished the raw material for the *orientalistes* of the nineteenth and early twentieth centuries. First in France, later in England and America, the taste for such creations grew by leaps and bounds, only to die out during the 1950s and 1960s. Since 1970, active collecting of this school by the oil-rich inhabitants of the Middle East has created a tremendous rise in prices.

Edwin Lord Weeks. *Camels Watering at an Oasis.* Oil on canvas, 39¼ x 76¾". The Forbes Magazine Collection, New York. As *Group of Camels Feeding, Morocco,* lot 257 in a sale of paintings, sketches, and drawings by the late Edwin Lord Weeks (1849–1903), American Art Galleries, March 15, 1905. It fetched $620.

Weeks's reputation was built on the romantic scenes of North African life he produced for his wealthy clients. Although he was born and continued to exhibit in the United States, Weeks was an inveterate traveler who sketched and wrote extensively during his journeys to Morocco, India, Persia, and other exotic locales.

Eugène Delacroix. *Arab Fantasia*. c. 1833. Oil on canvas, 24 x 29″. Städelsches Kunstinstitut, Frankfurt, Germany. Lot 70 in the auction of modern paintings collected by J. W. Kauffman of St. Louis, Missouri, conducted by the American Art Association on January 28, 1905.

Although works by the great painters of cattle pieces, Troyon and Van Marcke, brought the high prices at the Kauffman sale ($8,000 and $9,600, respectively), Delacroix's *Arab Fantasia* brought $2,100—a reasonable sum for the time.

The taste for "orientalist" paintings in France predated the American passion for such works by half a century. Delacroix (1798–1863) became one of the earliest and greatest masters of this genre after a trip to Morocco in 1832, when he filled seven notebooks with sketches of native life and scenery.

Hispano-Moresque blue-and-gold lusterware pottery dish. Catalan, late sixteenth century. Diameter 15¾″. Private collection.

Many pieces of this type were included in an auction of Hispano-Moresque pottery, the collection of Sarah B. Conkling, held at the American Art Galleries on February 9, 1905. The dish illustrated here brought $1,100* when sold at Sotheby Parke Bernet, New York, in 1981.

Hispano-Moresque pottery was originally produced by Arab artisans resident in Spain. After their expulsion in the fifteenth century, Spanish potters continued to produce wares influenced by the earlier tradition.

1906

Marie Curie becomes the first woman professor at the Sorbonne in Paris.

Paul Cézanne dies.

H.M.S. *Dreadnought,* **the world's first all-big-gun battleship, is launched by the British navy.**

Rembrandt Harmensz. van Rijn. *Portrait of Petronella Buys.* 1635. Oil on oval wood panel, 31 x 23″. Private collection, the Netherlands. Lot 50 in the auction of paintings from the estate of Joseph Jefferson, sold on April 27, 1906, at the American Art Galleries for $20,600. In October 1980, it was sold as part of the André Meyer collection, at Sotheby Parke Bernet, New York, for $990,000*.

"The Valuable Paintings Collected by the Late Joseph Jefferson" was the major auction of 1906. Anton Mauve's *Return of the Flock* brought $42,500—the high price of the sale—and respectable sums were paid for the other "modern" works that had belonged to a man who enjoyed a reputation as a painter as well as an actor.

Joseph Jefferson (1829–1905) was the fourth of his family and the third of his name on the stage. He was particularly identified with the role of Rip Van Winkle, a part he played hundreds of times on tour. He is quoted as having said, "No man is fit to live without a hobby; if it be for pictures, he's a happy man, but he will find it an expensive one."

1907

Madison Square, c. 1900. Behind the trees rises the tower of Madison Square Garden, designed by Stanford White in 1896.

The year got off to an auspicious start on January 25, when thirty "Masterpieces by the Men of 1830" (that is, Barbizon and kindred works by, among others, Théodore Géricault, J.-F Millet, Camille Corot, and Théodore Rousseau) belonging to H. S. Henry of Philadelphia, were auctioned for a total sale of $352,000. A *Return to the Farm* by Constant Troyon fetched $65,000, the evening's highest price, when dealer Herman Schaus outbid Senator William A. Clark of Montana.

But the auctions most people were talking about in 1907 were those held to liquidate the vast collections of the late Stanford White. White, born in New York in 1853, became one of the city's most prominent figures. Washington Arch, the Century Association, the Herald Building, and the numerous office buildings and residences done in association with his partners, C. F. McKim and W. R. Mead, made his name synonymous with the profession of architecture. His lavish home and extravagant life-style as well as his reputation as a bon vivant added to this professional celebrity, and when an allegedly wronged husband, Harry Thaw, shot him to death in the roof garden of Madison Square Garden, the entertainment complex White had designed in 1896, Stanford White and Evelyn Nesbit Thaw— the Girl in the Red Velvet Swing—became part of American popular legend.

The American Art Association sale was spread out over many sessions, beginning on April 4 with "artistic furnishings and interior decorations" (409 lots); continuing with "old and modern paintings" on April 11–12 (123 lots) and a supplementary sale of "valuable artistic property" on November 25–29 (651 lots); and concluding with "antique marbles and stone mantels" on December 10 (110 lots). There were frames White had designed for his artist-friends, antique statuary, Spanish altars, a dining-room ceiling, and potted rubber trees. Buyers included decorator Elsie de Wolfe, socialite Mrs. Stuyvesant Fish, playwright David Belasco, newspaper magnate William Randolph Hearst, and other notables who fought their way through the crowds of curious onlookers to bid on White's treasures. There was more than enough for everybody.

Albert Pinkham Ryder. *Pegasus.* c. 1883–87. Oil on wood panel, 12 x 11⅜". Worcester Art Museum, Worcester, Massachusetts. Lot 30 in the sale of Stanford White's paintings conducted by the American Art Association on April 11–12, 1907, at Mendelssohn Hall.

Pegasus, which brought $1,225, had been created for Charles de Kay, a prominent New York collector and writer on the arts. The title de Kay preferred was *The Poet on/Pegasus/Entering the Realm of the Muses.*

Albert Ryder (1847–1917) is one of the truly great painter-poet-eccentrics in art history. Wandering through the streets and parks of the city, he was a familiar sight to New Yorkers, and he became a cult figure in his later years, lionized by a younger generation of artists who included ten of his paintings in the 1913 Armory Show.

White's painting collection, which consisted of not very impressive Old Masters, plus some very fine American and European contemporary works, was not of as much interest to the public as were the lavish furnishings of his house at 121 East Twenty-third Street, where Baroque columns and rich tapestries created a palatial ambience.

Augustus Saint-Gaudens. *Diana*. c. 1891. Bronze, height 24⅞". National Museum of American Art, Smithsonian Institution, Washington, D.C. Gift of John Gellatly, 1929. Lot 364 in the Stanford White sale at the American Art Galleries fetched $300 on November 27, 1907.

Saint-Gaudens (1848–1907) did two versions of *Diana* for the tower of the new Madison Square Garden designed by Stanford White. This is a study for the first figure, which was made of copper, and which, after having been installed 347 feet above the ground (becoming the highest object in the city and one of the world's loftiest weather vanes!) was taken down and replaced when the architect and sculptor agreed that the eighteen-foot goddess was too large. Shown in 1893 at the World's Columbian Exposition in Chicago, the first *Diana* has disappeared.

The second version, only thirteen feet high, was installed in 1894 and remained in place until the Garden was demolished. It is now in the Philadelphia Museum of Art.

1908

No artist personifies the rise, fall, and rise again of American nineteenth-century painting better than Albert Bierstadt (1830–1902).

Born in Solingen, Germany, he arrived with his parents in New Bedford, Massachusetts, in 1832, and after preliminary artistic training in New England he traveled to Düsseldorf and Italy for further studies. He visited the American West in 1859, in 1863, and again in 1871, making hundreds of oil sketches of that still largely unspoiled region. Later, working from these, he painted the large studio canvases that brought him fame and prosperity.

Inspired by the imminent extinction of the American bison, and wishing to send a spectacular example of his work to the Paris Salon of 1889, held in conjunction with the Exposition Universelle, Bierstadt painted his enormous *Last of the Buffalo,* only to have it rejected by a jury of his fellow artists in New York as unfit to represent the United States in the exhibition. "Too large" and "not up to his best" were the proffered excuses, but, in fact, the taste of 1889—in tune with the Barbizon and Impressionist styles—found Bierstadt just too old-fashioned, an embarrassing anachronism to the younger generation. "It is a matter of indifference to me," the artist bravely insisted, "but I can not understand why they should refuse my picture. . . . I have endeavored to show the buffalo in all his aspects and depict the cruel slaughter of a noble animal now almost extinct." The painting was thought to have been sold for a large sum to a Col. J. T. North, but it certainly belonged to Edward Bierstadt, the artist's brother, in 1908, six years after the painter died, when an auction of the younger Bierstadt's collection was held at the American Art Association.

Albert Bierstadt's magnum opus has achieved a posthumous vindication. Its title, *The Last of the Buffalo,* was a very nearly accurate statement of fact: in 1889 there were only about 550 bison left in the United States. The picture was one of the factors that prompted the government to undertake a survey and plan of protection. Today there are more than 25,000 bison under government care.

Bierstadt's reputation, however, continued to decline for more than half a century after his death, with sales subsiding to what seem now to be ridiculously low levels. But, another belated triumph for Bierstadt occurred in June 1983, when a smaller version of *The Last of the Buffalo* brought $770,000* at a Sotheby Parke Bernet auction in New York.

Albert Bierstadt. *The Last of the Buffalo*. c. 1888. Oil on canvas, 71¼ x 119¼". Corcoran Gallery of Art, Washington, D.C. Gift of Mrs. Albert Bierstadt, 1909. Lot 75 in an auction of "Important Works in Oil Belonging to the Estate of the Late Edward Bierstadt," held at the American Art Galleries on January 22–23, 1908. Apparently Mrs. Bierstadt, the artist's widow (who was a millionaire in her own right), acquired it at the sale through an agent, for shortly thereafter she donated *The Last of the Buffalo* to the Corcoran Gallery. The price at the auction had been $1,100 to one D. P. Read.

1909

William Howard Taft is president of the United States.

Sergei Diaghilev organizes his Ballets Russes in Paris, with Michel Fokine as choreographer and Waslaw Nijinsky as lead dancer.

Lewis Hine's photographic journals dealing with child labor in America cause widespread consternation.

Ever since Japan was opened to trade with the West in 1854, interest had been growing in things Japanese, both in Europe and America. Sales of Japanese artifacts, usually organized by the Tokyo firm of Yamanaka, were annual events at the American Art Association for many years, beginning on January 11, 1893. Boston collectors, especially, were known throughout the world for their extensive holdings of Japanese swords, lacquer, ceramics, and paintings. Exhibitions of Japanese prints held in Paris from the 1860s on exerted a profound effect on many artists—Mary Cassatt, Paul Gauguin, Edgar Degas, J.A.M. Whistler, and William Merritt Chase, to name a few—and Japanese influence on early twentieth-century collecting in America is evidenced by three works of art sold at auction in 1909 and illustrated here.

The woodblock print by Katsushika Hokusai (1760–1849) was part of a sale devoted to Japanese prints, "Examples of the Popular School by Utamaro, Totokuni... and other Masters of 'Ukiyoe,'" as the Anderson Auction Company catalogue described them. Knowledge of Oriental art has increased markedly in the West since 1909, for today's bidders would know many more details than were given in that rather sketchy pamphlet about this print from the series *One Hundred Poems as Explained by the Nurse,* published in 1839, which suggests the beauty of maple leaves floating on the Tatsuta River.

William Merritt Chase. *The Kimono.* 1895–98. Oil on canvas, 35 x 45½". Thyssen-Bornemisza Collection, Lugano, Switzerland. Lot 62 in the sale of paintings that took place at Mendelssohn Hall and the American Art Galleries on March 11–12, 1909. The picture brought $260. The auction was held to "facilitate the settlement of the estate of the late James S. Inglis," who, with Daniel Cottier, had been a principal in Cottier & Company, leading art dealers in the city at the time.

William Merritt Chase (1849–1916), who met and painted with Whistler briefly about 1885, was a collector of Japanese and other exotic forms of art and bric-a-brac. *The Kimono* shows a Japanese painted paper screen as well as textiles and prints in the studio of the artist.

Katsushika Hokusai. *Ariwara no Narihira.* Colored woodblock print (*oban yoko-e*), 10¼ x 14½". Private collection.

Another example of this print was sold as lot 93 in the auction of "A Private Collection of Japanese Prints and Books," held by the Anderson Auction Company on Friday, December 17, 1909. There, it was called simply *Country Scene. Farmers and Tourists on a Bridge.*

The illustrated example sold for $2,090* at Sotheby Parke Bernet, New York, on May 13–14, 1983, and it was described then as having come from the Fichter Collection.

Jules-Joseph Lefebvre. *The Language of the Fan.*
c. 1882. Oil on canvas, 51 x 34½". The Chrysler
Museum, Norfolk, Virginia. Gift of Walter P.
Chrysler, Jr., 1971. Lot 98 in the James S. Inglis
estate sale at Mendelssohn Hall and the American Art Galleries on March 11–12, 1909.

Jules Lefebvre (1836–1911), a successful
French Salon painter, did a number of portraits
and studies of women in Oriental costume during the 1880s. Called *La Japonaise* in the Salon of
1883, this work, which fetched $460 at the
Inglis sale, had been titled *The Language of the
Fan* by 1909—and its new name attests to the
romantic and inscrutably mysterious qualities
attributed to the traditions and customs of Japan
by Western collectors.

1910

George V succeeds his father, Edward VII, as king of Great Britain.

Wassily Kandinsky paints what is considered to be the first abstract painting.

Jean Léon Gérôme. *Pygmalion and Galatea.* c. 1880s. Oil on canvas, 35 x 27″. The Metropolitan Museum of Art, New York. Gift of Louis C. Raegner, 1927. Lot 21 in the C. T. Yerkes sale on April 5, 1910, at Mendelssohn Hall went for $4,000.

Gérôme (1824–1902) executed a sculpture of this legend from Ovid's *Metamorphoses* about 1881, and the painting is thought to date from shortly thereafter. Depicted is the royal Cypriot sculptor Pygmalion being kissed by the statue of Galatea that has just come to life, thanks to the help of Aphrodite. George Bernard Shaw's *Pygmalion* and Lerner and Loewe's *My Fair Lady* are among the countless adaptations of the story that Gérôme has so appealingly captured in this painting.

Charles Tyson Yerkes (1837–1905) was for a time one of the world's most notorious and powerful tycoons. After gaining control of Philadelphia's horsecar lines, he moved on to Chicago, where he built that city's transit system and became known as the Traction King. By 1900 he was part of the syndicate that built London's underground railway. Wherever he went, Yerkes's financial wheeling and dealing, his corruption of the local officials who regulated the systems he controlled, his romantic involvements, his possessions, and his philanthropies captured the public's imagination. Theodore Dreiser's novel *The Titan* was based on Yerkes's career.

When he died, Yerkes's Fifth Avenue mansion and its contents were bequeathed to the citizens of New York, and funds were also earmarked for a hospital and for the Yerkes Observatory in Wisconsin. The great financier's estate turned out to be worth much less than had been thought, however, and eventually it was announced that *everything* would be sold: King Ludwig of Bavaria's bed, Old Master pictures, and fabulous carpets. The American Art Association sale attracted a distinguished crowd of bidders, including Mrs. Harry Payne Whitney and Captain J. R. De Lamar, both wealthy collectors who bought extensively. A Turner picture, *Rockets and Blue Lights* (now in the Sterling and Francine Clark Art Institute, Williamstown, Massachusetts), went to Joseph Duveen for $129,000—at that time the highest price ever paid in the United States for a picture at auction.

During Yerkes's life, he had a reputation as a lothario: his acknowledged mistresses as well as numerous "wards" and protégées both young and not so young were conveniently established in cities where he conducted business. Appropriately, the works from his estate sale chosen for illustration are all glorifications of the female form, one by a great sculptor of the Age of Reason, two others by painters of Yerkes's own era.

Jean Antoine Houdon. *Diana.* 1782. Bronze, height, including pedestal, 114″. The Huntington Library, Art Gallery, and Botanical Gardens, San Marino, California. Lot 247 in the Yerkes sale held April 11–13, 1910, at the Yerkes mansion. It was bought for $51,000 by Joseph Duveen.

This *Diana* was one of three bronze casts by the great Houdon (1741–1828) of a piece that was originally intended for Empress Catherine II of Russia. The second cast is in the Louvre, the third in the Musée des Beaux-Arts, Tours. The present example, for which Yerkes had paid $70,000, previously belonged to Sir John Scott, heir to Sir Richard Wallace, owner of the Château de Bagatelle, where the statue was originally placed.

William-Adolphe Bouguereau. *Invading Cupid's Realm (Le Guêpier).* c. 1892. Oil on canvas, 84 x 60″. Private collection. Lot 39 in the C. T. Yerkes sale on April 5, 1910, at Mendelssohn Hall. The price was $10,000.

When resold at Sotheby Parke Bernet, New York, in May 1983, this picture brought $412,500*. In both instances, the price established a world auction record for the artist. Bouguereau (1825–1895) was an academic painter and a notable teacher who enjoyed immense popularity during his lifetime.

1911

The dispersal of the library and art collection of Robert Hoe (1839–1909) during the years 1911 and 1912 brought to public attention the amazing breadth of the interests of this modest yet singularly able and brilliant man.

In 1886 Hoe took over the family printing business founded by his grandfather and developed it into an amazingly innovative and profitable operation. He is credited with the perfection of the rotary press, the high-speed web press, and reliable color presses, all of which revolutionized the printing of periodicals.

In a modest house on Manhattan's East Thirty-sixth Street, near the palatial residence of J. P. Morgan, Hoe amassed the largest private library in the United States. This amazing bibliophile, the founder of the Grolier Club, owned literally thousands of rare books, including medieval manuscripts, incunabula, many early printed books, folios of Shakespeare, and letters written by Christopher Columbus, Washington Irving, and Edgar Allan Poe.

Hoe, a founder of the Metropolitan Museum, was also an art collector, and in addition to an incredibly rich literary hoard, he left a most distinguished art collection, containing Chinese porcelains, Japanese netsukes and inros, Chelsea scent bottles, Lamerie silver, German stoneware, French furniture, and paintings.

In his will, Hoe authorized his executors to sell at auction all his personal property, including the artworks and books, and gave them instructions to "take expert advice and sell the same either in London or Paris or New York as they shall deem most advantageous," for, as he said, "if the great collections of the past had not been sold, where would I have found my books?"

The total receipts at the Hoe book auctions amounted to $1,932,056—a staggering sum then, and the greatest amount of money for any library sold at auction in the United States until 1969, when the Thomas Streeter book sales at Sotheby Parke Bernet, New York, totaled over $3 million.

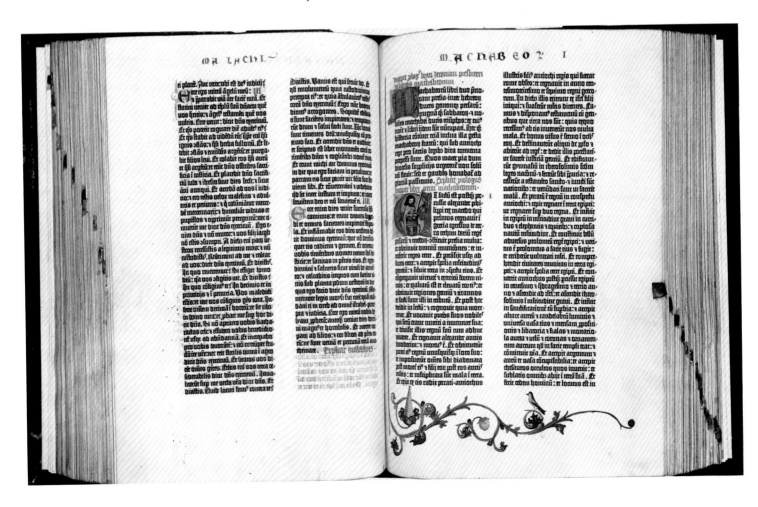

Opposite: Bible printed on vellum by Johann Gutenberg, c. 1455, at Mainz, Germany. The Huntington Library, Art Gallery, and Botanical Gardens, San Marino, California. Lot 269 in the first part of the Hoe book sale, conducted by the Anderson Auction Company from April 24 to May 5, 1911. The illustration shows the Bible open to a chapter from 1 Maccabees.

Auctioneer Sidney Hodgson of London was brought over to conduct the sale. The bidding began at $10,000, and up to $30,000 it was a three-way battle between the London book dealer Bernard Quaritch, Joseph Widener of Philadelphia, and G. D. Smith (bidding for Henry Huntington). After $30,000 it was Widener versus Huntington, until the latter became the successful bidder at $50,000—having offered the highest price ever paid at auction for a book.

The first extant book printed with movable type, and the first edition of the Latin Vulgate, Gutenberg's Bible (also called the Forty-two-line Bible) understandably follows the style and format of contemporary hand-lettered books. Printed initial letters were often illuminated by hand to enhance the effect.

It is generally thought by experts that about 35 copies of this Bible were printed on vellum, 150 on paper. Today 12 copies on vellum and 36 on paper are known to exist, all in collections in Europe and the United States.

Francesco di Stefano, called Pesellino. *Madonna and Child with Saint John.* c. 1455. Tempera on wood panel, 28½ x 21¼". The Toledo Museum of Art, Toledo, Ohio. Gift of Edward Drummond Libbey. Lot 97 (catalogued as by a follower of Filippo Lippi) in the sale of the art collection of Robert Hoe, held at the American Art Galleries on February 15, 1911. The painting went to the Blakeslee Galleries, New York, for $1,275.

1912

Arizona and New Mexico are admitted to the Union, making forty-eight states in all.

Woodrow Wilson is elected twenty-eighth president of the United States.

One early collector in the United States was an internationally famous emigré and resident of New Jersey known as the Comte de Survilliers. In reality he was Joseph Bonaparte (1768–1844), elder brother of Napoleon, who, after serving as the French minister to Parma and Rome and helping to negotiate a treaty with the United States, became successively king of Naples and king of Spain.

He was a failure in both of these royal posts but did manage to assemble a small collection of pictures, which he took with him to America after his forced abdication. From 1815 to 1841 he lived mainly in Bordentown, New Jersey, on the banks of the Delaware River, not far from Philadelphia. On September 17, 1845, a Philadelphia auction firm held a sale of "paintings and statuary" at Joseph Bonaparte's mansion. The 128 lots included pictures by Claude-Joseph Vernet (several of which are now in the Pennsylvania Academy of the Fine Arts), a still life by de Heem, and a still life of flowers catalogued as by van Os. The purchaser of this last work is not known, but the painting appeared at auction in 1912, where it was again sold as a work by Jan van Os.

When the painting was consigned to auction for a third time, in 1979, scholarship dictated a reattribution to Jan Brueghel the Elder (1568–1625). It is now recognized as one of a group of related flower pieces all showing the same characteristic arrangement of blooms in a glass vase.

Today the ascription to Brueghel seems so obviously correct that it is hard to understand why van Os was once considered the painter, but in the nineteenth century the vogue for floral still lifes by this eighteenth-century artist was sufficient to incline collectors to attribute flower paintings to him rather than to Brueghel.

Opposite: Jan Brueghel the Elder. *A Still Life of Flowers.* c. 1610. Oil on copper, 13¾ x 10½". Private collection. Lot 487 (described as a work by Jan van Os) in the auction of the J. Hampden Robb collection, American Art Association, April 24–26, 1912, fetched $45.

When this painting was sold (as by Jan Brueghel the Elder) in an auction of Old Masters held at Sotheby Parke Bernet, New York, on January 12, 1979, it brought $451,000*.

United States establishes a federal income tax through final approval of the Sixteenth Amendment to the Constitution.

"International Exhibition of Modern Art" (Armory Show) is held in New York City.

The sale of Old Master and modern paintings collected by Matthew Chaloner Durfee Borden stands out as a major event at the American Art Association in a year chiefly characterized by some thirty auctions of Oriental art, Napoleana, samplers, prints, and the "embellishments of a residence."

The Borden sale included Dutch and Flemish Old Masters, English School portraits and landscapes, Barbizon paintings, plus a few unusual choices such as works by Greuze, Alma-Tadema, and Daumier. The highest price of the sale, $130,000, was paid for Rembrandt's *Lucretia* (now in the National Gallery, Washington, D.C.), and two of the English pictures brought over $100,000. For the "modern" works bidding was more moderate, and the audience gathered in the grand ballroom of the Plaza Hotel on St. Valentine's Day must have been surprised when a picture of poor people crowded into a railway car, by an artist whose work was not widely known or particularly fashionable at that time, fetched the highest price of the evening: $40,000.

Honoré Daumier (1808–1879) is something of an enigma among painters whose work has found favor with twentieth-century collectors. Caricaturist, political activist, lithographer, satirist, and loner, Daumier could not, and still does not, fit easily into one of the neat categories where painters are placed for the sake of convenience. Yet his paintings and drawings dealing with the daily life of urban people, the follies of amateur collectors, the venality of attorneys, and the life of Don Quixote have found their way into virtually every major collection of modern art, including the superb group of paintings by the Impressionists, their precursors, and their successors in the H. O. Havemeyer Collection at the Metropolitan Museum of Art. There hangs Daumier's *Third-Class Carriage*—one of the artist's finest works.

Louisine Havemeyer had become acquainted with the artist's work during her many visits to Paris, where a small group of influential collectors owned paintings by him. Among these connoisseurs was Henri Rouart, whose dozen paintings by Daumier had been sold at auction in 1912 for good prices. Then, too, Mrs. Havemeyer had the advantage of Mary Cassatt's knowledge and advice, and she, like the other Impressionists, admired Daumier's powerful art.

The Third-Class Carriage captures the loneliness and quiet resignation of these early victims of mass transit. In her memoirs Mrs. Havemeyer recounts an experience in such a railway carriage, observing that "the poor are good-natured and kind-hearted, and their pleasant chatter, where it did not rise to the confusion of a din, was not disagreeable." As the Borden sale catalogue pointed out, "Every one of the faces seen in the background is markedly individualized. The handling is vigorous, and the picture has great beauty of tone and color." Not mentioned was what for us is one of the picture's most intriguing features: the pencil lines visible just beneath the surface of the paint. This is now understood to be the grid system Daumier employed to enlarge the painting from the watercolor version now in the Walters Art Gallery, Baltimore.

Figure of a Warrior. French, early seventeenth century. Bronze, height 8¼". Private collection. Lot 51, Rita Lydig collection sale, American Art Association, April 4, 1913.

In 1913 this figure, catalogued as *A Gladiator* done in the manner of Domenico Poggini, brought $725. In December 1982, the piece was sold at auction in New York at Sotheby Parke Bernet. This time it was identified as one of a group of warrior figures, probably of French origin. The price then was $19,800*.

Honoré Daumier. *The Third-Class Carriage*. c. 1863–65. Oil on canvas, 25¾ x 35½″. The Metropolitan Museum of Art, New York. Bequest of Mrs. H. O. Havemeyer, 1929. The H. O. Havemeyer Collection. Lot 76 in the sale of "Notable Paintings Collected by the late M. C. D. Borden, Esq.," held in the Plaza Hotel, February 13 and 14, 1913. It was bought by the firm of Durand-Ruel, possibly the agent for Mrs. Havemeyer, for $40,000.

1914

Assassination of Austrian archduke Franz Ferdinand precipitates World War I.

Published this year are Booth Tarkington's *Penrod*, E. R. Burroughs's *Tarzan of the Apes*, and Robert Frost's *North of Boston*.

"I do not paint poor boys because the public likes them and pays me for them, but because I love the boys myself, for I was once a poor lad." So read the artist's words on the title page of the catalogue that accompanied the auction sale entitled "The Finished Pictures and Studies Left by the Late J. G. Brown, N.A.," published by the American Art Association in 1914.

John George, or, as he is usually referred to, J. G. Brown (1831–1913) arrived in the United States from England in 1853, when he was twenty-two, and within a few years he was exhibiting smallish genre scenes of well-behaved and well-dressed children at the Brooklyn Art Association.

Gradually he evolved a formula for success to which he was faithful until his death: the sentimental portrayal of the mudlarks, toughs, bootblacks, and other children forced to play or make a living on the sidewalks of New York City. It has been estimated that in the late nineteenth century tens of thousands of urchins eked out a homeless existence in Manhattan and Brooklyn, taking whatever odd jobs might be available, shining shoes, hawking newspapers, carrying packages, or running errands. At night they slept in cellars and on steam grates, or—if they had six cents to pay for a bed—in a newsboys' lodging house, where they were warned that "boys who swear and chew tobacco cannot sleep here."

Jacob Riis, the great chronicler of the miseries of New York's slums, shocked America with the tragedy of these children's lives in his *How the Other Half Lives,* of 1890. But J. G. Brown was no Jacob Riis of the easel, nor was he by any stretch of the imagination an American Daumier. He idealized and sentimentalized these ragged boys and girls so that his portrayals were entirely fit to hang in the galleries of the city's rich collectors.

Brown's children are invariably clean, healthy, happy, and good-hearted. *The Gang,* for example, barely hints at the havoc actually caused by the gangs of toughs who terrorized the citizenry. *The Sidewalk Dance,* painted in front of Brown's own Forty-second Street residence, conjures up the lilting strains of "East Side, West Side, all around the town." These are two of Brown's most unsentimental titles; most, like *Be Mine* and *Old Friends Must Part,* are maudlin.

The sale, reflecting Brown's popularity, was considered successful. One of the most enthusiastic buyers was the food-packing magnate H. J. Heinz of Pittsburgh. Prices for Brown's pictures plummeted in the 1920s, however, and did not recover until a renewal of interest in American genre painting began in the mid-1960s.

Wedgwood blue-and-white jasper-ware medallion of Terpsichore, the Muse of Dance and Choral Song. Late eighteenth century. Height 3¼". Private collection.

A similar medallion was included in an auction of the Townsend collection of "Beautiful Old Wedgwood," sold at the American Art Association on February 16, 1914, for $52.50. Many such specialized sales were held at an early date in the firm's history. It should also be noted that the tradition of collecting Wedgwood pottery in America is of long standing.

Opposite above: John George Brown. *The Sidewalk Dance.* c. 1894. Oil on canvas, 40¼ x 60". Private collection. Lot 153 in the artist's estate sale, held at the American Art Galleries on February 9–10, 1914. It reappeared at a Sotheby Parke Bernet auction in New York on April 25, 1980, when it sold for $115,500*. In 1914 the price was $730.

Opposite below: John George Brown. *The Gang.* Oil on canvas, 40 x 60". Private collection. Lot 154 in the artist's estate sale held by the American Art Association on February 9–10, 1914, brought $800. When the oil was sold at Sotheby Parke Bernet, New York, on October 22, 1981, this same painting brought $82,500*.

1915

Cunard liner *Lusitania* is sunk by Germany, bringing protest from the United States.

***Of Human Bondage* by W. Somerset Maugham is published.**

Filet lace tablecloth. Venice, seventeenth century. 64 x 45″. Lot 169 in an auction of "Costly Tapestries, Beautiful Old Laces, Antique Brocades and Velvets... from the Collection of the Duc d'Avray, Paris," held at the American Art Association on January 22. The selling price was $400.

The market was active for rare old textiles during the first half of this century, and a large number of auctions were devoted exclusively to them. Fine household linens and laces were an important feature of virtually every single-owner collection sale, even more so if it were held on the premises of a great house. Lace had its own terminology, history, romance, and price structure based on design, workmanship, age, and country of origin.

Interest in laces and table linens fell as social conditions after World War II brought servantless homes and increasingly less formal lifestyles. Today, laces at auction are occasional curiosities, not the avidly collected staple commodities of the salesroom they once were.

1916

James Joyce's *A Portrait of the Artist as a Young Man* is published.

Armored tanks are introduced by the British on the Western Front.

Rasputin is assassinated in St. Petersburg, Russia.

Maiolica "oak-leaf" jar. Florence, mid-fifteenth century. Height 7½". Private collection. Lot 664 in the Volpi–Davanzati Palace sale, American Art Association, November 21–25, 1916. The price was $300.

Although America had not as yet formally entered the Great War, several auctions of 1916 were the indirect result of the battles then raging on the European continent. On January 25, novelist Edith Wharton organized a benefit sale for refugees. Later, after a summer when his American customers for the most part stayed at home, Elia Volpi, an Italian dealer, whose extensive holdings of Renaissance works of art were housed in the famous old Davanzati Palace in Florence, sent a boatload of treasures to New York.

The highest price of the Volpi–Davanzati Palace sale was $66,000, paid by Joseph Widener of Philadelphia for a bronze incense burner by Riccio. There were also bronze, ivory, and terra-cotta sculptures, Savonarola chairs, cassones, armor, pictures, and textiles—as well as an extensive collection of maiolica, the brilliantly painted tin-glazed earthenware produced in Italy from the fifteenth century onward that reflects so well developments in European decorative design and changes of taste through the years.

Most intriguing of all the ceramics was a little bowl correctly identified in the catalogue as a piece of Medici porcelain—the first produced in Europe, under the patronage of the Medici dukes at Florence. At the Volpi–Davanzati Palace auction the piece was probably sought after more as an object associated with the great Medici family than as a documentary example in the history of Western ceramics. Only about sixty pieces made at the Medici factory are known to exist; all have Chinese-style blue-and-white decoration and either a drawing of the Florentine Duomo or the six balls of the Medici coat of arms on the bottom. When "rediscovered" in 1973, this little bowl made a huge price advance from its modest showing in 1916.

Another notable auction of 1916 was occasioned by turmoil in the American silk industry. In better days, a mill owner with the unlikely name of Catholina Lambert had built himself a castle on Garret Mountain, overlooking Paterson, New Jersey, America's first industrial city, and had adorned it with an enormous art collection that included Old Master, American, Barbizon, and Impressionist paintings. Lambert had been forced to mortgage the paintings after a millworkers' strike in 1912–13 had beggared him, and in 1916 the Paterson Safe Deposit and Trust Company ordered their sale at an auction managed by the American Art Association.

The Old Masters did reasonably well, with a Luini altarpiece selling for $33,500. But it was the moderns who carried the day. Examples by Blakelock, Alexander H. Wyant, Winslow Homer, Pierre Puvis de Chavannes, and Pierre Auguste Renoir brought figures in excess of $15,000, and the Pissarros, Sisleys, Monets, and Monticellis fetched only slightly lesser prices. Blakelock's *Brook by Moonlight* set an auction record for an American painting: $20,000.

The silk industry has long since disappeared from Paterson, and Bella Vista Castle is now the home of the Passaic County Historical Society. But whenever one of the pictures from the Catholina Lambert sale appears at auction, the provenance instantly indicates to seasoned gallery-goers former ownership by a very astute and quite adventurous industrialist, whose crenelated hilltop home contained one of the most unusual collections of old and modern masters ever assembled in America.

Blue-and-white Medici porcelain bowl. Florence, late sixteenth century. Diameter 5⅛". Private collection, Europe. Lot 625 in the sale of the Volpi-Davanzati Palace collection, American Art Galleries, November 21–25, 1916. The bowl, which realized $200 then, later entered the collection of William Boyce Thompson of Yonkers, New York, whose house eventually became part of Elizabeth Seton College. That institution sold the bowl at auction in New York, at Sotheby Parke Bernet, on November 1, 1973 (lot 130), at which time it brought $180,000.

Adolphe Joseph Thomas Monticelli. *Cupid's Offering*. 1860. Oil on canvas, 36 x 23½". The Fine Arts Museums of San Francisco. Mildred Anna Williams collection. Lot 165 in a sale of "Valuable Paintings and Sculpture by the Old and Modern Masters, forming the Catholina Lambert Collection," managed by the American Art Association, grand ballroom of the Plaza Hotel, February 21–24, 1916. It brought $2,025. *Cupid's Offering* was one of twenty-nine Monticellis in the Lambert sale, two of which had been commissioned by the Empress Eugénie of France. Such a large number of works by one artist prompted a special essay in the catalogue, where the tragic career of Monticelli (1824–1886) was recounted in great detail.

1917

Czar Nicholas II of Russia is forced to abdicate; Alexander Kerensky establishes a moderate government.

Piet Mondrian and Theo van Doesburg found *De Stijl*.

Among the interesting auctions of 1917 were the Anderson Auction Company's January 22 sale of the Arnold Genthe collection of four hundred Japanese prints, and the American Art Association's sales of the Frederick B. McGuire collection of bronzes by Barye and Mène (February 26), Thomas B. Clarke's Americana (May 22), and James ("Diamond Jim") Brady's "Costly Furnishings" (October 22).

William Merritt Chase's studio sale was, however, of still greater significance, standing as a dramatic record of the life, career, and wide-ranging tastes of a man who dominated the American art scene for many years: as painter, teacher, collector, and vivid personality. Included in the May auction were numerous pictures by Chase himself, works by his friends and fellow artists, and many unusual objects that had adorned his studio—furniture, textiles, fans, ceramics, and sculpture acquired over the years and often used as "props" in his paintings. Prices were generally quite low, probably due to the complete involvement—after April 6—of the United States in the Great War, then raging in Europe.

William Merritt Chase. *The Artist's Daughter in Her Mother's Dress.* c. 1899. Oil on canvas, 60 x 36⅛". Hirshhorn Museum and Sculpture Garden, Smithsonian Institution, Washington, D.C. As *Young Girl in Black,* lot 190 in the Chase studio sale, held by the American Art Association on May 14–15, 1917. The price at the auction was $90.

Thomas Eakins. *Sailing.* 1874. Oil on canvas, 32 x 46⅜". Philadelphia Museum of Art. Alex Simpson, Jr., Collection. Lot 245 in the auction of William Merritt Chase's collection by the American Art Association on May 14–15, 1917, brought $310.

Opposite: Claude Monet. *Pleasure Boats at Argenteuil.* c. 1875. Oil on canvas, 21½ x 26". Private collection. Lot 138 in a sale held by the American Art Association at the Plaza Hotel on January 16–17, 1917. Included were twenty-four Monets from the collection of the late James F. Sutton, co-founder of the Association. Lot 138, which brought $4,500 in 1917, fetched $1.43 million* when it was sold at Sotheby Parke Bernet, New York, in 1981. Number 143 in the sale, *View of Bordighera,* brought $15,900— the auction record for a Monet until 1957!

Proposed Arcade Railway under Broadway, View near Wall Street. Lithograph in colors by Ferd. Mayer & Sons and Melville C. Smith, Projector. c. 1870. Private collection.

This is another impression of the print that was lot 114 in the Percy Pyne II sale, held at the American Art Association on February 5–7, 1917. Pyne, whose townhouse on Park Avenue is now the Center for Inter-American Relations, was a great collector of American prints. This print, which brought $90 at the Pyne sale, depicts an early plan to relieve traffic congestion on lower Broadway. A trial stretch—New York's first subway—extending from Murray Street to Warren Street was opened in February 1870.

By the early twentieth century, many notable New Yorkers began forming collections of views and printed records of the monuments of old New York, for, as the city rapidly expanded, almost all of the relics of the seventeenth, eighteenth, and early nineteenth centuries were destroyed through redevelopment.

1918

Although the gargantuan auction (over 2,000 lots) of George A. Hearn's collection of paintings and decorative arts was the most important sale of the year, the Bardini and the Brady collection auctions provided plenty of excitement as well. In the Hearn dispersal, Inness's *Wood Gatherers,* for which the merchant-collector had paid $5,600 at the Clarke sale of 1899, made $30,800—a new record for any American painting sold at auction.

More controversial and adventurous acquisitions were available in a sale held by the American Art Association's chief rival. Newly relocated in a grandiose building at Park Avenue and Fifty-ninth Street, which had been the meeting hall of a German cultural society, the Anderson Galleries put on public view what were probably the first Cubist paintings ever sold at auction in the United States—and perhaps anywhere.

Dr. R. M. Riefstahl, in his prefatory note to the catalogue, described the consignor, Mr. Léonce Alexandre Rosenberg, as a prominent connoisseur and dealer in works of art, whose collections ranged from early Egyptian art, to Chinese ceramics of the Han Dynasty, to Persian miniatures, to modern paintings. All these categories were represented in the auction catalogue, notably an important picture by Paul Signac, two works by Pablo Picasso, two by Auguste Herbin, nine by Juan Gris (1887–1927), six by Diego Rivera (at that time still a Cubist painter), and sculptures by Henri Laurens and Jacques Lipchitz. "So far as we know," the catalogue pointed out, "this is the first time that characteristic pictures of this [Cubist] school have been put to the acid test of a public sale." And strong acid it was, for the prices, by today's standards, were embarrassingly low: the Signac brought $300, a Maurice Denis picture $600, a Picasso $20, a Rivera $40 (bought by John Quinn), and a Lipchitz carved wood sculpture of a seated woman $10.

The man who had assembled this group of things, Léonce Alexandre Rosenberg, was the son of a dealer in antiquities and modern paintings. He decided to concentrate on the works of the Cubists after the war and opened his Galérie de l'Effort Moderne in Paris, which became a leading outlet for advanced art, rivaling the gallery of Daniel Henry Kahnweiler for some time.

Mitchell Kennerly, the president of the Anderson Galleries, was a champion of modern art in America, and it was no doubt his willingness to take a flier that brought Rosenberg's collection to his firm for auction.

Joseph Bail. *The Cook's Helper.* Oil on canvas, 32 x 23½". Private collection. Lot 43 in the sale of paintings from the collection of James Buchanan Brady held at the American Art Association on January 14, 1918.

Brady, known as "Diamond Jim" because of his collections of jewels, is traditionally associated with the self-indulgent, somewhat scandalous life-style of an avowed hedonist. His collection of paintings, however, displays a preference for traditional cattle scenes, pastoral landscapes, and harmless genre pieces like this work by the French artist Joseph Bail (1862–1921), which fetched $300.

Juan Gris. *Still Life with Playing Cards.* 1916. Oil on canvas, 28¾ x 23⅝″. Washington University Gallery of Art, St. Louis, Missouri. Lot 94–B in the sale of selections from the Léonce Alexandre Rosenberg collection, Anderson Galleries, May 3, 1918. The catalogue entry read, "Modern Oil Painting–Still Life: Playing cards, glass, chessboard on a table; painted on canvas signed Juan Gris 8–16. Framed. Height 30 inches, width 25 inches." The price was a mere $32.50.

Donato di Niccolò Bardi, called Donatello. *The Virgin and Child with Two Angels.* Painted terracotta, arched top, 35 x 28″. Private collection. Lot 351 in the sale of the "Beautiful Treasures and Antiquities…belonging to the famous expert and antiquarian, Signor Stefano Bardini, of Florence, Italy," held at the American Art Galleries on April 23–27, 1918. It sold for $4,200.

The Bardini auction was one of the biggest and best of the many sales held during the war and postwar years at which staggering quantities of Italian Renaissance furniture and works of art passed into American private collections. Much of this material is now in museums. The Bardini collection brought $443,790 for almost 800 lots. The catalogue's preface noted that the owner's decision to sell was "due to the disturbed state of his country."

1919

Eighteenth Amendment to the United States Constitution (Prohibition) is ratified; bootleggers begin their operations and federal agents enforce the law.

Treaty of Versailles officially ends World War I; League of Nations is established at Geneva, Switzerland.

Walter Gropius establishes the Bauhaus school at Weimar, Germany.

Ando Hiroshige. *A Sudden Shower at Ohashi Bridge.* Nineteenth century. Colored woodblock print *(oban),* about 15 x 10". Private collection.

Another impression of this print was lot 569 in the sale of Japanese colored prints belonging to Judson D. Metzgar of Moline, Illinois, held at the American Art Association on May 15–16, 1919. It was knocked down at $42.50. Examples of this print have sold during the years that followed at prices ranging from $100 (in 1947) to $2,400 (in 1971) to $15,950* (on June 26, 1981, lot 333).

Japanese artworks, including prints, continued to be regular features of the auctions at both the American Art Association galleries and the Anderson Galleries throughout the first decades of the twentieth century.

Petit-point embroidery of the Adoration of the Magi. English, first quarter of the seventeenth century. Silk, silver, and silver-gilt thread on canvas, 10½ x 12½″. The Metropolitan Museum of Art. Gift of Irwin Untermyer, 1964. Lot 942-D in the auction of "Rare and Beautiful Textiles and Embroideries of the Widely-Known Connoisseurs and Experts, Vitall and Leopold Benguiat of New York and Paris, now discontinuing their Paris and New York establishments." The sale took place at the American Art Association on April 11, 1919. The price for this embroidery, praised in the catalogue as "of the utmost rarity and historic interest," was $350.

The Benguiats organized dozens of sales of carpets, tapestries, textiles, and antiquities during the first decades of the twentieth century at the American Art Association.

Raoul Larche. *Venus Rising from the Waves*. Late nineteenth century. Gilt bronze, height 29″.

Another cast of this bronze was lot 630 in the J. R. De Lamar house sale, conducted by the American Art Association on November 20–22, 1919, and it fetched $630. The illustrated example was sold at Sotheby Parke Bernet, New York, on November 12–13, 1980, for $11,000*.

On November 20–22, 1919, the American Art Association held a sale of the contents of this mansion at 233 Madison Avenue, New York City, the home of Captain J. R. De Lamar. The magnificence of the house was matched by the opulence of its furnishings. Today the building, designed in 1905 by C. P. H. Gilbert, houses the Polish Consulate.

Opposite: Great Mosque Carpet of Ardebil (detail of the central medallion). Persian (Tabriz), 1540. Silk and wool, 23′6″ x 13′. The Los Angeles County Museum of Art. Gift of J. Paul Getty. Lot 446 brought $57,000 in the sale of the furnishings of the home of Captain J. R. De Lamar, held on the premises by the American Art Association on November 20–22, 1919.

This somewhat controversial rug is a pendant to and counterpart of a famous carpet in the Victoria and Albert Museum, London, which is dated 946 A.H. (A.D. 1536). Before the Great Mosque Carpet of Ardebil appeared at the 1910 Yerkes sale, only the London example was publicly known; apparently, parts of the Yerkes rug had been cannibalized to restore the London carpet. J. K. Mumford, a contemporary authority on the subject, observed that "in view of what has been accomplished, it is an open question whether the relic here displayed . . . is not . . . the more interesting fabric of the two."

1920

The auction year began with the sale of Captain De Lamar's paintings (January 29); continued with Raoul Tolentino's Italian furniture (April 16); and drew to a close with H. J. Heinz's Oriental art (December 14)—all at the American Art Association. Two interesting Anderson Galleries sales were "Ninety-six Drawings by Renoir" on April 16, and the relatively avant-garde print sale selectively illustrated here. The market for etchings by J.A.M. Whistler and J.-F. Millet was strong during the early twentieth century. Prices for most works by the later French school of artist-printmakers remained relatively low.

James Abbott McNeill Whistler. *The Piazzetta.* 1880. Etching, third state of five, 10 x 7⅛″.

An impression of the first state of *The Piazzetta* brought $135 at the Anderson Galleries sale of prints on May 28, 1920. On November 13, 1981, the example illustrated here brought $4,400* at Sotheby Parke Bernet, New York.

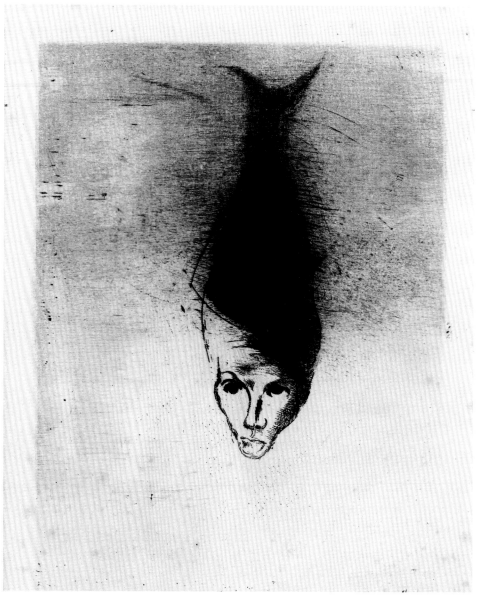

Jean-François Millet. *The Gleaners.* c. 1855. Etching, second state of two, c. 7½ x 10″.

Lot 146 in a sale of prints at the Anderson Galleries on May 28, 1920, was another example of the second state of *The Gleaners.* In November 1982, the impression illustrated here brought $3,740* at Sotheby Parke Bernet, New York.

Odilon Redon. *Sciapode.* 1892. Etching, 8 x 5¾″.

An example of this print was lot 76 in the May 28, 1920, sale at the Anderson Galleries. It was part of a rather unusual group consigned by the noted critic, connoisseur, and art dealer Marius de Zayas that included prints by Matisse, Toulouse-Lautrec, Degas, Derain, and Gauguin.

The *Sciapode* brought only $5 in 1920. In 1975, another example of this etching by Redon brought $900 at a Sotheby Parke Bernet auction in New York.

1921

Hilaire Germain Edgar Degas. *Madame René De Gas*. 1872–73. Oil on canvas, 28⅝ x 36¼″. National Gallery of Art, Washington, D.C. Chester Dale Collection. Lot 51 in the auction of pastels and paintings by Degas held by the Paris dealer Georges Seligmann, American Art Association, January 27, 1921. It sold for $17,000 and was catalogued simply as *Portrait of a Woman in White*.

In 1872–73 Degas (1834–1917) visited his brother, a cotton broker in New Orleans. Several of the artist's most striking works date from this brief sojourn in America, among them this touching portrait of the artist's blind sister-in-law. The success of this auction was an indication of Degas's popularity among American collectors.

One of the most important auctions of medieval, Gothic, and Renaissance works of art ever held in America took place this year when stockbroker Henry C. Lawrence's collection of rare and marvelous objects was consigned to the American Art Association. Rarest and most desirable of all were the splendid stained-glass panels Lawrence had acquired from some of Europe's most respected dealers.

Joseph Duveen (bidding for Philadelphia collector Joseph Widener) and William Randolph Hearst (bidding for himself) were expected to carry off most of the finest pieces. However, on the afternoon of the auction a mystery bidder outshone (and outbid) the two old pros. When lot 372, the Tree of Jesse Window, was put on the block, a tall young stranger astounded the audience by paying $70,000 for this masterpiece of medieval glass. The young man, Raymond Pitcairn of Bryn Athyn, Pennsylvania, proceeded to buy twenty-three of the stained-glass panels in the Lawrence collection for $153,850 in all—a lot of money in the salesrooms of 1921, but by no means out of the question for the heir to the Pittsburgh Plate Glass Company fortune.

After the auction Pitcairn took the panels home to Bryn Athyn, where he was erecting a Gothic-style cathedral as the headquarters of the Church of the New Jerusalem, which followed the teachings of Emanuel Swedenborg. The windows were not intended for the church itself, but were acquired in order to serve as models and sources of inspiration for the artisans working on the building's modern glass.

In later years Pitcairn continued to acquire significant works of art of the Middle Ages, including many stone architectural fragments, but the stained-glass panels purchased on that Friday afternoon in 1921 remained his outstanding acquisitions. The Lawrence sale was, literally, a "once in a lifetime" opportunity. Raymond Pitcairn rose to the occasion.

Marsden Hartley. *The Aero*. c. 1914. Oil on canvas, 42 x 34½" (including painted frame). National Gallery of Art, Washington, D.C. Andrew W. Mellon Fund, 1970. Probably lot 46 *(Pre-War Pageant)* in the auction of paintings by Marsden Hartley at the Anderson Galleries on May 17, 1921, at which time it sold for $40.

The artist had organized the sale with the help of Mitchell Kennerly and Alfred Stieglitz, Hartley's dealer, whose own gallery was located in the Anderson Galleries building at the time. The proceeds from the auction of the 117 paintings allowed Hartley to return to Europe for further travel and study. *The Aero* was in the collections of artists Hamilton Easter Field and Robert Laurent before it was acquired by the National Gallery.

Ash-wood armchair. Philadelphia, c. 1790. Height 35¼". Philadelphia Museum of Art. Bequest of Marie and Fiske Kimball. Part of lot 99 of the Shippen-Burd collection of family heirlooms, sold at the American Art Galleries on March 7–8, 1921, for $4,000.

The Shippens and the Burds, two old Philadelphia families, were related through marriage. In the catalogue of the sale, this chair, together with eleven other chairs and a settee, were identified as "The Marie Antoinette Drawing-Room Suite, Louis XVI Period of the Sixteenth [*sic*] Century." Later, when the French tapestry coverings were removed, the furniture was discovered to be of Philadelphia, not of Paris, origin.

Federal carved mahogany card table. American, early nineteenth century, possibly by Duncan Phyfe. Height 29⅜". Yale University Art Gallery. The Mabel Brady Garvan Collection. Lot 655 in the auction of American furniture and decorative objects sold by Louis Guerineau Myers of New York, American Art Galleries, February 24–26, 1921. It fetched $800.

A pair of tables of almost identical design was sold in New York at Sotheby Parke Bernet in June 1983 for $275,000*.

Interestingly, the 1921 auction catalogue placed great stress on the political implications of the carving as symbolic of the triumph of the American eagle over the British lion in the War of 1812. Louis Myers, associated with the Rockefellers, was a pioneer aficionado of Americana in the 1920s, along with Henry Francis du Pont and Francis P. Garvan.

King from the Tree of Jesse Window, Soissons Cathedral. France, c. 1210–15. Pot-metal glass, 30½ x 31½". The Glencairn Museum, Bryn Athyn, Pennsylvania. The Raymond Pitcairn Collection. Lot 372 in the Henry C. Lawrence sale, American Art Association, January 27–29, 1921, sold for $70,000.

The window was originally installed in the Cathedral of St. Gervais and St. Protais at Soissons about 1210, and it had somehow survived the damage inflicted on the church by the Huguenots, the Revolutionaries, warring armies, and an explosion, only to be sold off in the late nineteenth century, when the windows were restored and "reorganized." Described in the Lawrence catalogue as "English, thirteenth century," the *King* from the Tree of Jesse Window is now acknowledged to be one of the finest examples of French stained glass in America.

Emperor Theodosius on Horseback from the Legend of the Seven Sleepers of Ephesus Window, Rouen Cathedral. France, c. 1210. Pot-metal glass, 24½ x 27⅞". The Metropolitan Museum of Art, New York. Cloisters Collection.

This panel, although not in the Lawrence sale, is from the same Seven Sleepers series as three others that Raymond Pitcairn acquired at the 1921 auction.

The story, told in *The Golden Legend,* relates how seven early Christian brothers evaded execution through divine intervention by sleeping, rather than being suffocated, after their hiding place in a cave was sealed up by order of the Roman emperor.

1922

King Tutankhamen's tomb is unearthed by British archaeologist Howard Carter.

Paul Cézanne. *Still Life with Apples.* c. 1885–98. Oil on canvas, 27 x 36½". The Museum of Modern Art. Lillie P. Bliss Collection. Lot 156 in the sale of modern pictures belonging to "the widely known antiquarian Dikran Khan Kelekian of Paris and New York," held on the evenings of January 21 and 22, 1922, in the Plaza Hotel's grand ballroom. The painting brought $21,000—an outstanding price for a Cézanne. In fact, it was at that time the highest price ever reached at auction for a work by this enigmatic genius who has come to be recognized as the great master of modern art.

Dikran Khan Kelekian, generally called "Papa," was a dealer who had long been acknowledged as a great authority on Oriental and ancient art. Born in Turkey of Armenian parents, he served as an honorary Persian consul (whence the title "Khan") and had become an outspoken devotee of modern art. In the words of Frank Crowninshield, he "befriended any and every discouraged artist who came to him for solace, encouragement, or aid."

In 1922 Kelekian decided to hold an auction of his extraordinary collection of modern art under the aegis of the American Art Association, and so his Derains and Matisses, van Goghs and Dufys were sold—some for what appear now to be extremely low prices, others so high for the time that the more conservative salesroom observers were shocked.

Vuillards, Vlamincks, Dufys, and Utrillos brought prices in the low hundreds. But John Quinn bought a Cézanne landscape for $9,500 and Seurat's *Woman Powdering Herself* (now in the Courtauld Institute, London) for $5,200. The high price of the evening was $21,000, paid by Lillie P. Bliss for Cézanne's great still life illustrated here. Miss Bliss was to become one of the co-founders and principal benefactors of New York's Museum of Modern Art, which opened in 1929 at Fifth Avenue and Fifty-seventh Street.

Kelekian died in 1952, just a few years before his enthusiasm for the Postimpressionists and the School of Paris masters was taken up in force by a generation that would pay millions for the works of Cézanne.

1923

Earthquake kills 100,000 people in Tokyo and Yokohama.

Henry Ford sells 2 million low-priced Model T cars in the United States.

Caruso as Canio in *Pagliacci*. Photograph by Mishkin.

This photograph may well show the singer dressed in what was lot 879 in the auction of his collection on March 5, 1923, described in the American Art Association catalogue as "opera costume for the character of 'Canio'...consisting of tan smock and trousers trimmed with black and rosettes, tan lawn ruff,...one pair of tan canvas shoes with black and tan rosettes." One of more than fifty lots devoted to operatic items, the outfit brought $25.

The Caruso auction was one of the last conducted by the aging Thomas E. Kirby. At the outset the whole audience rose for a minute of silent prayer in tribute to the great Metropolitan Opera tenor who had won the hearts of New Yorkers as no other opera star ever had. It was a fitting finale for the virtuoso auctioneer who had dominated the New York auction scene for four decades.

Blue-and-white porcelain dish. Chinese, Ming Dynasty (fifteenth century). Diameter 13⅛″. Private collection, Hong Kong. Lot 1088 in a sale of Chinese porcelains from the collection of William Rockefeller held at the Anderson Galleries on November 19–24, 1923. The dish was catalogued as of the Qianlong period (1736–95) and the price it fetched was $6. When resold at Sotheby Parke Bernet, New York, in May 1980, it was recognized and properly listed as early Ming. Its price, $83,600*, was indicative of today's preferences in Chinese ceramics.

The more expensive pieces in the Rockefeller sale were single-color porcelains. For example, $1,300 was paid for an apple-green jar of the Kangxi period (1662–1722). This reflected the era's taste for later and more colorful ceramics.

Enrico Caruso. *Caricature Self-Portrait*. India ink, 18 x 18″. Lot 1165 in the auction of the antiques, costumes, coins, books, and drawings belonging to the late Enrico Caruso, held at the American Art Association's new galleries at 30 East Fifty-seventh Street, New York, on March 5, 1923. The caricature sold for $55.

1924

By Act of Congress, all native-born American Indians are declared United States citizens.

Calvin Coolidge is elected president of the United States.

André Breton's first Surrealist Manifesto is published.

No fewer than fifteen auctions of fine prints were held at the American Art Association and the Anderson Galleries in 1924, a figure indicative of the very active market for etchings and engravings at the time.

Print sales were often held in conjunction with rare-book sales during the 1920s, and the same scholarly approach to collecting characterized both fields. In fact, many of the people interested in books also collected prints.

Color and size of prints were not nearly as important to collectors then as they are now. Instead, the intricacy of the composition, the brilliance of the impression, and the reputation of the etcher or engraver in the current ranking of favorites governed the market.

Old Master prints were highly regarded, of course, but the graphic work of certain leading contemporary figures such as Sir Francis Seymour Haden (1818–1910), Joseph Pennell (1860–1926), and James McBey (1883–1959) fetched extraordinary prices. The market later slumped badly, only to recover selectively in recent years.

Sir Francis Seymour Haden. *Sunset in Ireland.* 1863. Drypoint. Second state of two, 5½ x 8½".

A "trial proof" impression of this print was lot 238 in the sale of the M. D. Noe collection on November 12, 1924, at the American Art Association. In 1982, *Sunset in Ireland* brought $880* at a Sotheby Parke Bernet print sale in New York.

Red-figure column krater. Greek (Attica), c. 470–460 B.C. Height 15½". The Cleveland Museum of Art, Cleveland, Ohio. Gift of Mrs. Leonard C. Hanna, 1924. Lot 62 in an auction of antiquities and Renaissance art from the firm of C. & E. Canessa held at the American Art Association on January 25–26, 1924. The price realized was $950.

This Greek vessel in which wine was mixed with water, typical of black-ground pottery of the fifth century B.C., is inscribed *Simonos* ("Simon," a common name) beneath the rim.

Félix Buhot. *Une Jetée en Angleterre*. 1879. Etching, drypoint, aquatint, and roulette. Second state of four, 11¾ x 8".

An impression of this print was lot 145 in the auction of Buhot etchings from the collection of Miss Myrtilla Daly Noe of Bayonne, New Jersey, sold at the American Art Association on November 12, 1924. In November 1981, the illustrated example brought $1,870* at a Sotheby Parke Bernet print auction in New York.

Félix Hilaire Buhot (1847–1898) is best known for his mysterious landscapes and scenes of Paris.

1925

F. Scott Fitzgerald's *The Great Gatsby,*
Theodore Dreiser's *An American Tragedy,*
and Franz Kafka's *The Trial* are published.

Crossword puzzles and dancing the
Charleston become popular in the United
States.

Jean Baptiste Camille Corot. *Saint Sebastian
Tended by the Holy Women.* c. 1874. Oil on canvas, 51½ x 33¾". National Gallery of Art, Washington, D.C. Timken Collection, 1959. Lot 68
in the Arthur Tooth collection auction at the
American Art Association on February 19,
1925.

The canvas sold for $17,600, a reasonable but
unspectacular price for the work of Corot
(1796–1875), an artist who had been extremely
popular among American collectors for
decades. So sought after were his paintings, in
fact, that the market was always well supplied
with fakes, copies, and doctored-up pastiches,
prompting a famous aphorism of the day,
"Corot painted 4,000 pictures, 20,000 of which
are in America."

Corot's stature has stood the test of time,
although the silver-toned landscapes favored by
early collectors have been superseded in popular taste by his figure subjects and the Italian
scenes of his youth. An earlier version (1853) of
the Saint Sebastian theme is in the Walters Art
Gallery, Baltimore, Maryland.

Opposite: Joseph Wright of Derby. *Maria and
Her Dog Sylvio.* 1781. Oil on canvas, 63 x 45½".
Derby Art Gallery, Derby, England. Lot 69 in
the sale of paintings belonging to the late
Arthur Tooth, held at the American Art Association on February 19, 1925, to liquidate the
stock of the New York branch of the London
dealers Arthur Tooth & Sons   sold for $650.

The subject is taken from *A Sentimental Journey* by Laurence Sterne (1713–1768), and this
picture was first exhibited at the Royal Academy in 1781. Joseph Wright of Derby
(1734–1797), a respected portraitist and the British master of *chiaroscuro,* never achieved the
popularity and price levels in America that his
contemporaries, the fashionable "phiz-
mongers" Sir Joshua Reynolds and George
Romney enjoyed.

1926

United States Marines are sent to Nicaragua to put down an uprising.

Gertrude Ederle becomes the first woman to swim the English Channel.

George III satinwood and mahogany marquetry commode. English, late eighteenth century. Height 33″. Private collection. Lot 99 in the Leverhulme furniture sale on February 9–13, 1926, at the Anderson Galleries. The price of this chest of drawers was $5,200; a matching piece (lot 99-A) brought $4,500.

The commodes were resold as a pair at Sotheby Parke Bernet, New York, in 1973 for $42,000.

This year was one of the greatest ever for auctions of all sorts. At the American Art Association a copy of the Gutenberg Bible from the Austrian abbey of Melk brought $106,000; Senator William A. Clark's collection of pictures and furniture was auctioned in January, allowing the curious to see how the most ornate mansion on Fifth Avenue had been furnished; and the studio sale of the American Impressionist J. Francis Murphy (1853–1921) gave eager collectors of his autumn landscapes a chance to bid on some of his finest works.

But the most important and memorable sale of the year was the dispersal at the Anderson Galleries of the paintings and sculpture, furniture and art objects collected by England's recently deceased Viscount Leverhulme. The viscount, who had been born plain William Lever, amassed a fortune from his soap business, Unilever Brothers, Ltd., and left an immense collection and a million dollars in death duties to be paid. The executors of his estate were persuaded by Mitchell Kennerly of the Anderson Galleries to take advantage of the strong market for things English in America. The Earl of Mayo tried to stop the export of these British treasures from England. However, Cortlandt Field Bishop was even more upset that this great assemblage of fine and decorative arts was not to be sold at his American Art Association. He accused Kennerly of stabbing him in the back and wrote to his associates Hiram Parke and Otto Bernet, "We need publicity, we cannot get enough of it, but Kennerly has stolen a march on us."

The Leverhulme auctions were highly successful and they brought in almost $1.25 million. They are remembered to this day by students and collectors of English furniture and decorative arts.

Hepplewhite inlaid and painted mahogany and satinwood secretary. English, late eighteenth century. Height 95¾″. The Metropolitan Museum of Art, New York. Gift of Irwin Untermyer, 1956. Lot 301 in the Viscount Leverhulme sale (Part I), Anderson Galleries, February 9–13, 1926. When this large and handsome desk was resold as part of the Genevieve Garvan Brady collection at "Inisfada," Manhasset, Long Island, in 1937, it brought $480.

1927

Joseph Stalin achieves full power in the USSR; Leon Trotsky and his followers are expelled from the party and country.

Charles Lindbergh makes his historic solo flight from New York to Paris.

Gwen John. *Woman Reading at a Window.* 1911. Oil on canvas, 16½ x 10″. The Museum of Modern Art, New York. Mary Anderson Conroy Bequest in memory of her mother, Julia Quinn Anderson. Lot 465 in the John Quinn sale at the American Art Association on February 9–12, 1927. It brought $600.

Almost certainly a self-portrait by the sister of the famous portraitist Augustus John, this was the first of many paintings Quinn purchased from Gwen John (1876–1939). The two eventually became great friends. In 1914 Quinn wrote to the artist, "Your little picture of the girl reading is invariably picked out in my apartment and immensely admired."

John Quinn (1870–1924) was doubtless one of the most influential figures of the early twentieth century in the fields of arts and letters. As a lawyer for Thomas Fortune Ryan, the Copper King, Quinn became a wealthy man in his own right and was able to devote his energy and money to politics, the support of Irish nationalism, and the patronage of the leading young writers of Ireland and England. About 1910 he became interested in modern European and American art and was instrumental in putting together the International Exhibition of Modern Art, held at the Sixty-ninth Infantry Regiment Armory in New York City in 1913 (the famous Armory Show). He bought important works from the show and began to visit the leading galleries of New York and Paris, buying continually from them and directly from the artists until his last illness. The extent of his interests and the number of great works owned by Quinn are amazing. Brancusi, Braque, Cézanne, Derain, Duchamp-Villon, Dufy, Gauguin, Gris, Hartley, Augustus and Gwen John, Matisse, Picasso, Redon, and Rouault were all represented in his collection. Two of the twentieth century's best-known paintings were once his: *The Sleeping Gypsy* by Henri Rousseau (Museum of Modern Art, New York) and *The Circus* by Georges Seurat (Musée du Louvre). In addition, Quinn formed a magnificent collection of books and manuscripts. Other major accomplishments of this lawyer-collector were the reform of U.S. Customs regulations on the importation of sculpture, and a role in arranging for the publication of T. S. Eliot's *The Waste Land* in *The Dial* magazine in 1922.

After Quinn's death, the executors of his estate gave his papers to the New York Public Library and made plans to liquidate the art collection. However, uncertainty as to the best means caused confusion and delay. Art critic Henry McBride wrote in *The Dial,* "The perfectly obvious procedure would have been to have sold the pictures and carvings at public auction last winter [1924–25] in New York. . . . The time was ripe and the stage was set. . . . It is well known to students of auctions that the excitement of them [is] cumulative and the atmosphere of a big sale breeds a frenzy of buying that ensures success . . . of course, there were dealers to advise the executors . . . against a sale last winter. There were other experts who thought certain works . . . could only be sold in Paris." Mentioning the educational value of a big auction to the public, McBride concluded that, this chance having been missed, the Quinn affair was "doubly tragic." Many of the most important works were sold privately, and an auction of the lesser property followed in 1927.

Walt Kuhn. *The Tragic Comedians.* c. 1916. Oil on canvas, 95½ x 45″. Hirshhorn Museum and Sculpture Garden, Smithsonian Institution, Washington, D.C. Lot 516 in the auction of the John Quinn collection of modern art, held at the American Art Association galleries, February 9–12, 1927. The picture fetched $80.

The American artist Walt Kuhn (1880–1949) and John Quinn had been acquainted with each other since before the Armory Show of 1913. This major work, showing the influence of the French and German avant-garde, was exhibited at the Montross Gallery, New York, in 1917, together with recent paintings by Arthur B. Davies, Jules Pascin, Charles Sheeler, and Max Weber.

1928

Herbert Hoover is elected president of the United States.

Aldous Huxley's *Point Counter Point* and Evelyn Waugh's *Decline and Fall* are published.

Thomas Gainsborough. *The Harvest Waggon.* c. 1784–85. Oil on canvas, 48 x 59". Art Gallery of Ontario, Toronto. Gift of Mr. and Mrs. Frank P. Wood, 1941. Lot 30 in the "Sale of the Painting Collection of Judge Elbert H. Gary," held by the American Art Association at the Plaza Hotel on April 20, 1928. The price was $360,000, which remained the record for any painting sold at auction in America until 1961. *The Harvest Waggon* had been purchased by the Prince of Wales, later George IV, directly from the artist and was given by him to Mrs. Fitzherbert.

Auctions of note held at the American Art Association and Anderson Galleries during the year 1928 included A. Conger Goodyear's paintings, Mrs. William Saloman's French art, and Lyman Bloomingdale's paintings. The year's major auction event, however, was the sale of art collected by the late Elbert H. Gary (1846–1927). Usually referred to as Judge Gary, for he was a member of the judiciary in Illinois for a time, Elbert Gary helped form the United States Steel Corporation in 1901 with J. P. Morgan, and was chairman of its board of directors for many years. The company town of Gary at the site of U.S. Steel's major mill in Indiana was named for him, but his longstanding and outspoken opposition to labor reform provoked widespread criticism.

Like many millionaires of the period, Gary moved to New York and began collecting art in a big way. His interests were divided between French decorative arts and more or less traditional Old Masters and English pictures, with a sprinkling of such conservative "moderns" as Fritz Thalow, a Norwegian Impressionist whose works were much in vogue.

On the evening of the painting sale, the audience of prominent collectors included Governor Fuller of Massachusetts, Joseph Widener, theater-manager Edward F. Albee, Henry Walters, and circus magnate John Ringling. English portraits did well, and Thomas Gainsborough's charming *Harvest Waggon* surged to a record price. No Gainsborough was to bring more until 1960. The decorative-arts sale was also a great success, and the figure of $245,000 paid by Mrs. Edward S. Harkness for a Houdon bust of Sabine remained the highest auction price for a sculpture until the 1960s.

Louis XV oak and mahogany veneered marquetry table, with the stamps of the *ébénistes* Jean-François Oeben and Roger Vandercruse, called Lacroix. French, eighteenth century. Height 27½". The Metropolitan Museum of Art. Jack and Belle Linsky Collection, 1982. Lot 271 in the sale of Judge Gary's furniture and decorative arts, held on April 19 and 20, 1928, at the American Art Association's galleries. The table was bought by Joseph Duveen for $71,000. In 1971 it was sold again, at Sotheby Parke Bernet, this time as part of the collection of Martha Baird Rockefeller. The magnitude of the price—$410,000—was due almost as much to its distinguished provenance as to its superb craftsmanship and exemplary design. The original owner was the Marquise de Pompadour, favorite of Louis XV of France, and patron of the leading artists and craftsmen of the mid-eighteenth century.

1929

Ernest Hemingway's *A Farewell to Arms*, Robert Graves's *Goodbye to All That*, and Erich Remarque's *All Quiet on the Western Front* are published.

Mention of the final year of the Roaring Twenties reminds most people of the Wall Street Crash, which began on October 23. But to veteran connoisseurs of American antiques, 1929 is more happily remembered for the concurrence of two major events, the Reifsnyder auction in April, and the Girl Scout Exhibition in September-October.

Ever since the 1876 Centennial Exposition in Philadelphia, interest in the arts and crafts of Colonial and early Federal America had been growing slowly but steadily, and it was further stimulated by the Hudson-Fulton celebration in New York in 1909. Furniture and decorative objects began to be recognized as works of art, not just relics of the early English settlement of North America. Scholars began to unearth the names of cabinetmakers, silversmiths, and limners. In 1924 the Metropolitan Museum opened its American Wing; in 1926 John D. Rockefeller began to restore the historic colonial city of Williamsburg, Virginia; and in 1929 noted collector Louis G. Meyer, treasurer of the Rockefeller Foundation, working in collaboration with other collectors, organized a show at the American Art Association to benefit the Girl Scouts. American eighteenth- and nineteenth-century furniture was the focal point of the show, but paintings, glass, ceramics, and silver were featured as well. It was the first big loan exhibition of its type since the Hudson-Fulton Celebration Exhibition. While the exhibition was still being planned, the sale of the collection of Howard Reifsnyder was announced.

The foreword to the Reifsnyder catalogue, written by one "privileged to inspect, detail by detail, the beauty and the astounding preservation of the large collection," expressed the hope "that the dispersal of the magnificent collection of Philadelphia furniture formed by the late Mr. Howard Reifsnyder of Philadelphia over a period of thirty years will coincide with the beginning of a new epoch in the history of the appreciation of American craft-products." There followed a synopsis of the story of American Colonial furniture-making and then a description of the 717 lots, which proceeded to set one price record after another during the four days of the auction.

Henry du Pont, the most active buyer at the sale, purchased what one noted authority, Joseph Downs, has called "the highest development of the Philadelphia Chippendale School of Furniture"—the Van Pelt Highboy. It is now one of the glories of the museum founded by du Pont at Winterthur, Delaware.

These two events marked the association of big prices and big names with *American* decorative arts—rather than European antiques—for the first time in a highly visible way. For this reason the Girl Scout Exhibition and the Reifsnyder sale are still hailed as landmarks in the history of collecting in the United States.

Blued, silvered, and gilt steel parade armet. North Italian, c. 1590. Height 11¾". The Metropolitan Museum of Art, New York. Fletcher Fund, 1929. Lot 239 in the sale of the collections of Count Pepoli and others at the American Art Association on January 18–19, 1929. It brought $7,200. This extraordinary parade helmet was made to resemble a fantastic bird's head in the tradition of antique Roman armor. Although never a major part of the business, sales of arms and armor were held with some regularity from the 1920s on.

Chippendale carved mahogany highboy (Van Pelt Highboy). Philadelphia, c. 1765–80. Height 90½". ©The Henry Francis du Pont Winterthur Museum, Winterthur, Delaware. Lot 696 in the Howard Reifsnyder auction of Colonial furniture, held at the American Art Association on April 24–27, 1929. A magnificent example of Philadelphia craftsmanship, the chest is named after the original owners. It brought $44,000, the highest price of the Reifsnyder sale and the record auction price for a piece of American furniture until 1970.

Maurice Prendergast. *Salem, Massachusetts*. Watercolor, 11½ x 19″. Lot 397 in the auction sale of the art collection of noted American artist Arthur B. Davies at the American Art Association on April 16–17, 1929. Then it fetched $400; in 1983 this watercolor was sold at Sotheby Parke Bernet, New York, for $24,200*.

Chippendale carved mahogany wing armchair, by Benjamin Randolph and Hercules Courtenay. Philadelphia, 1770–72. Philadelphia Museum of Art, Philadelphia, Pennsylvania. Purchased: Museum Fund, 1929. Lot 674 in the Howard Reifsnyder auction at the American Art Association, April 24–27, 1929. The price, $33,000, was an acknowledgment of the excellent craftsmanship and importance of the makers: Benjamin Randolph and Hercules Courtenay, cabinetmaker and master carver, respectively. Although the chair reflects the most elaborate type of English rococo design, extensive research by leading authorities before and since the Reifsnyder sale has established a Philadelphia origin for the piece. It is one of six "sample chairs" that descended in the Randolph family and were thus attributed to Benjamin Randolph alone in 1929.

The American Art Association–Anderson Galleries during the Girl Scout Loan Exhibition, held September 25–October 9, 1929. The draped brown wall coverings seen here were the distinctive background for every subsequent exhibition at the 30 East Fifty-seventh Street galleries.

1930

Hawley-Smoot Tariff, designed to protect American industry, aggravates the world-wide economic depression.

Edward Hopper paints *Early Sunday Morning* and Grant Wood paints *American Gothic*.

The effects of the Wall Street Crash of 1929 were not felt immediately in the salesroom—at least not as regards important pieces of Americana then being bought by such wealthy collectors as Henry du Pont, John D. Rockefeller, and Francis P. Garvan. The Philip Flayderman sale included two such examples that illustrate how provenance and documentation reinforce beauty and condition in establishing a price at auction.

The table and the strainer illustrated here could both be traced back to Jabez Bowen, a prominent figure in Colonial Rhode Island and a member of the Council of War in 1781. In addition, letters referring to the table established the date and authorship of the piece: Newport, June 30, 1763, John Goddard, cabinetmaker.

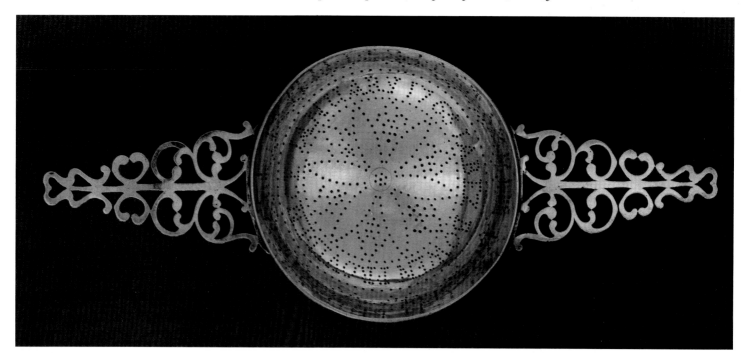

Silver punch strainer, made for Jabez Bowen by Jonathan Clarke. Boston or Salem, Massachusetts, 1765. Length 11⅞". Yale University Art Gallery, New Haven, Connecticut. The Mabel Brady Garvan Collection. Lot 388 in the Philip Flayderman sale, January 2–4, 1930, at the American Art Association–Anderson Galleries.

The well-known Rhode Island silversmith Jonathan Clarke (c. 1705–1770) noted his patron's name and residence and the date in tiny perforations around the floral motif in the bowl of the strainer, which was purchased for $5,500 in 1930.

Chippendale carved mahogany tea table, made for Jabez Bowen by John Goddard. Newport, Rhode Island, 1763. Height 27". ©The Henry Francis du Pont Winterthur Museum, Winterthur, Delaware. Lot 450 in the sale of the Philip Flayderman collection of American furniture realized $29,000 at the American Art Association–Anderson Galleries on January 2–4, 1930.

Mary Cassatt. *Girl Arranging Her Hair.* 1886. Oil on canvas, 29½ x 24½". National Gallery of Art, Washington, D.C. Chester Dale Collection. Lot 75 in the auction of paintings and violins from the H. O. Havemeyer estate, held at the American Art Association–Anderson Galleries on April 10, 1930.

Girl Arranging Her Hair was exhibited by the artist in 1886, in the eighth Impressionist group show, where it won high praise, even from such a hard-to-please critic as Degas, who is alleged to have exclaimed on seeing it, "What style!" He bought the picture and it was included in the Degas estate auction in Paris in 1918, where it was acquired by Mr. and Mrs. Havemeyer, longtime friends and patrons of both Degas and Cassatt.

Girl Arranging Her Hair brought $4,600 at the Havemeyer sale, but another painting by Cassatt, also bought by Chester Dale, fetched $8,500, the highest auction price for a work by the artist up to that time.

1931

Japanese invade Manchuria.

World's two tallest structures are completed in New York: the Chrysler Building and the Empire State Building.

The Road, Winter. 1853. Hand-colored lithograph by O. Knirsch, published by N. Currier Company, New York. 17¼ x 26⅛". Private collection.

Illustrated here is an example of the Currier print *The Road, Winter,* which was lot 209 in the Francis P. Garvan sale of Americana at the American Art Association–Anderson Galleries on January 8–10, 1931, and which sold for $700. Another version of this print (which depicts Currier himself in the sleigh) was sold at Sotheby Parke Bernet, New York, in November 1971, at which time it brought $2,700.

The Depression eventually began to affect even the clients of the American Art Association–Anderson Galleries. Sales declined both in number and in profitability, but Americana continued to inspire solid if unspectacular bidding. Benjamin Flayderman and Israel Sack—two widely known New England dealers—held interesting auctions in New York of American furniture, as did the respected collector Francis P. Garvan. Prints, especially those by Currier and Ives, were now taken seriously as collectors' items.

There were also auctions of American etchings, books, silver, and furniture. Collectors of American glass helped to swell interest and prices, and two astute pioneer collectors, George S. and Helen McKearin, wrote books that are still the standard works of reference in the field. The early sales of objects from the McKearin collection were accompanied by catalogues that served as helpful tools for budding collectors in a newly developing area of expertise.

This was very much in the tradition of the American Art Association and the Anderson Galleries, which had always aimed to provide as much information as possible in the auction catalogues they published for prospective bidders' use.

Looking at some of the early catalogues, with their lengthy descriptions and critical comments, their explanatory essays and often flowery biographies and prefaces, today's sophisticated reader may be tempted to smile condescendingly. But it must be remembered that the profusion of textbooks, colorplates, coffee table books, museum catalogues, and art magazines we take for granted did not exist in those days. The auction catalogue was, and continues to be, an educational as well as a selling tool.

THE ROAD, - WINTER.

An assortment of early American glass from the Mr. and Mrs. George S. McKearin collection was consigned for auction at the American Art Association–Anderson Galleries on April 22–23, 1931, and January 6–7, 1932. Several pieces attributed to the glass factory of Henry William ("Baron") Stiegel (1729–1785) at Manheim, Pennsylvania, were included. A blown, pattern-molded, amethyst glass "perfume flask" like the one in the center of the top shelf in the picture brought $300 at the 1931 sale. In the Helen Janssen Wetzel auction conducted at Spring Township, Pennsylvania, by Sotheby Parke Bernet in September 1980, a similar example brought $2,420*.

Queen Anne burl-walnut long-case clock, works by Daniel Quare and Stephen Horseman. London, c. 1715. Height 78¼". The Metropolitan Museum of Art, New York. Gift of Irwin Untermyer, 1964. Lot 1233 in the dispersal of the collection of David Belasco, held at the American Art Association–Anderson Galleries on December 8–12, 1931. It sold for $2,300. Daniel Quare is among the best of the English horologers. He took Stephen Horseman as a partner in 1709.

David Belasco (1853–1931) was a noted American playwright and theatrical producer. Two of his plays, *Madame Butterfly* and *Girl of the Golden West,* were adapted by Puccini into operas. The Belasco Theater still stands in New York City.

1932

In 1932 two distinguished members of the English aristocracy decided to consign some of their heirlooms to the American Art Association–Anderson Galleries for sale in New York, persuaded to some extent by the salesmanship of the New York concern's London representatives, who were attempting to compete aggressively against the firm's British auctioneer-rivals.

Philip Henry Kerr, marquess of Lothian, lecturer, writer, diplomat (in 1939 he was made British ambassador to Washington), needed to raise money for death duties on the properties that he had inherited in Norfolk and in Scotland. When, after lengthy secret negotiations, a sale in New York was announced, the British press and public proclaimed themselves "much upset," to which the marquess replied, "One has to get the best market for the things one is obliged to sell." In New York a lavish catalogue was produced and distributed, and on the night of the auction all the great book collectors were represented in the salesroom. The bidding of the inveterate bibliophile and owner of the American Art Association–Anderson Galleries, Cortlandt Field Bishop, together with generous bids of book dealers Dr. A. S. W. Rosenbach and Gabriel Wells, assured a successful sale. The grand total was $410,545—well above expectations.

In the spring, the marchioness of Curzon sent over pictures, tapestries, textiles, and gold boxes from her collection at Kedleston in Derbyshire, and George C. W. Fitzwilliam of Peterborough, Northamptonshire, consigned the so-called Olive Branch Petition (it brought $53,000). This amazing document, dated July 8, 1775, now in the New York Public Library, was a last-ditch appeal by members of the American Colonies' Second Continental Congress to George III for understanding and reconciliation in an attempt to avoid war.

François Boucher. *Venus Consoling Love*. 1751. Oil on canvas, 42⅛ x 33⅜". The National Gallery of Art, Washington, D.C. Gift of Chester Dale. Lot 80 in the sale of the collection of the marchioness of Curzon, of Kedleston, Derbyshire, at the American Art Association–Anderson Galleries on April 22, 1932. The price: $31,000.

Boucher, Madame de Pompadour's favorite artist, painted this picture for the king's mistress in the year she moved into a new apartment on the ground floor of the north wing at Versailles. It has been suggested that the marquise herself may have been the model for Venus, but her presence is more likely to have been allegorical: the court poets never ceased comparing the royal favorite with the goddess of love.

Psalter, manuscript illuminated on vellum by Prior John Tickhill, Priory of Wyrkesopp Monastery, Nottinghamshire. English, c. 1310. 155 leaves, each 12¾ x 8¾". The New York Public Library. Spenser Collection. Lot 7 in the auction of manuscripts and incunabula from the libraries of the marquess of Lothian, held at the American Art Association–Anderson Galleries on January 27–28, 1932. This important Latin psalter, "a monument of early English art," in the words of the catalogue, went to Dr. A. S. W. Rosenbach, the preeminent American book dealer, for $61,000. Shown here is folio 51, recto.

1933

Adolf Hitler becomes chancellor of Germany and begins a period of oppression and rearmament.

Joseph Stalin's purges of Communist Party members begin in Moscow.

President Roosevelt holds the first of his "fireside chats" on the radio.

Thomas Fortune Ryan (1851–1928) was a spectacularly successful financier. In 1886 he formed what is generally considered to be the first holding company—an incredibly useful device that he employed in connection with the then-profitable New York City transit system. He helped to organize a number of financial institutions as well as the American Tobacco Company, and he advised the king of Belgium on developing the Congo.

During the course of his long, busy, and lucrative career, Ryan bought antique works of art—many from the major auction houses—and paintings, sculpture, and prints by the leading artists of the day. The results were impressive. Etruscan bronzes, Limoges enamels, Renaissance sculptures, superb tapestries, and modern art filled the Ryan house at 858 Fifth Avenue. As Leslie A. Hyam, then a cataloguer for the American Art Association–Anderson Galleries and later president of Parke-Bernet, observed in his foreword to the Ryan catalogue: "A great collection of the works of different ages is...a complex chord of varied emotions, harmonized by the eye of the observer. More soberly it is a synthesis of the history of human feeling. Such a collection is that of Thomas Fortune Ryan, which covers in one form or another almost the entire period of post-Hellenic creative art...almost every historic impulse of the human spirit."

Francesco da Laurana. *A Princess of the House of Aragon*. 1472–75. Marble, height 17½". National Gallery of Art, Washington, D.C. Andrew W. Mellon Collection. Lot 416 in the dispersal of the T. F. Ryan collection at the American Art Association–Anderson Galleries on November 23–25, 1933. Joseph Duveen paid $102,500 for this Renaissance bust, the highest price of the sale.

Right: Auguste Rodin. *Saint John the Baptist Preaching.* 1878. Bronze, height 78¾". The Museum of Modern Art, New York. Mrs. Simon Guggenheim Fund.

A smaller bronze cast of *Saint John the Baptist* was included as lot 251 in the T. F. Ryan sale at the American Art Association–Anderson Galleries on November 23–25, 1933, and it brought $1,500. Ryan was a great patron of Rodin and he presented a group of marble sculptures by the artist to the Metropolitan Museum of Art. Rodin himself presented the Metropolitan Museum with a bronze portrait bust of Ryan, their mutual benefactor, in 1911.

Above: Joaquín Sorolla y Bastida. *The Wounded Foot.* 1909. Oil on canvas, 43 x 39". The J. Paul Getty Museum, Malibu, California. Lot 274 in the Thomas Fortune Ryan sale, November 23–25, 1933, American Art Association–Anderson Galleries brought $1,500.

J. Paul Getty acquired twelve of the twenty works by the Spanish artist Sorolla (1863–1923) in the Ryan sale. Sorolla enjoyed enormous popularity during the first decades of the twentieth century, especially in America. He exhibited often in Boston, Buffalo, and Chicago, and also in New York, where the Hispanic Society commissioned him to do a series of gigantic murals representing the Spanish provinces. In recent years, works by the artist that appear at auction in the United States have been purchased for the most part by Spanish collectors.

1934

Prohibition came to an end late in 1933, and leading off the parade of auctions in the newly "wet" but otherwise grim Depression year of 1934 was the sale of Edith Rockefeller McCormick's art collection in New York.

Mrs. McCormick was a daughter of John D. Rockefeller and daughter-in-law of Cyrus McCormick, the Reaper King. A social leading light, she was also a noted philanthropist, a student of the Swiss psychiatrist Jung, and a truly regal personality. Even when she dined alone, her menus were printed in French with gold ink on special paper by a small multigraph press used only for the purpose.

Less than two years after Mrs. McCormick's death, her executors put the property of this proud possessor up for sale. Some nine hundred of the choicest lots were sent to the American Art Association–Anderson Galleries, where they were described in an impressive catalogue complete with colored photoengravings. The silver, tapestries, magnificent laces and linens, furs, Chinese jades, and French furniture fetched a grand total of $330,000.

Two weeks later the contents of Mrs. McCormick's huge stone mansion on Lake Shore Drive in Chicago were auctioned in situ. Household objects and a Rolls-Royce were included in what amounted to one of the greatest auction dispersals in America—unrivaled until 1975, when the extensive collections of Mrs. McCormick's cousin Geraldine Rockefeller Dodge were sold by Sotheby Parke Bernet, New York.

Late Gothic verdure tapestry. Tournai, c. 1525. Wool, 11'2" x 19'2". The Art Institute of Chicago. Gift of the Antiquarian Society through the Jessie Landon Fund. Lot 909 in the Edith Rockefeller McCormick sale at the American Art Association–Anderson Galleries on January 2–6, 1934, brought $5,400.

This magnificent textile was illustrated in color in the catalogue (a rare event in those days) so as to show to best advantage the extraordinary design of animals and exotic birds gamboling amid flowers and lush green foliage typical of the so-called verdure tapestries woven at or near Tournai in Flanders during the sixteenth and seventeenth centuries.

Woman, attributed to Severo da Ravenna. Padua, sixteenth century. Bronze, height 7¼". Private collection. Lot 816 in the sale of the collection of Mrs. Benjamin Stern, held at the American Art Association–Anderson Galleries on April 4–7, 1934. Catalogued as a work by the Paduan sculptor Andrea Briosco, called Il Riccio, it brought $575.

When it was resold at Sotheby Parke Bernet, New York, in 1980, the bronze brought $30,800*.

1935

President Roosevelt's New Deal social programs, such as the Works Progress Administration, the Soil Conservation Service, and the Social Security system, continue to help lessen the effects of the Depression in the United States.

John O'Hara's *Butterfield 8* and Maxwell Anderson's *Winterset* are published.

Cortlandt Field Bishop (1870–1935) was heir to several old New York family fortunes, including that of Peter Lorillard, a manufacturer of snuff and tobacco, who was considered the first American millionaire.

After receiving a degree from Columbia University Law School, Bishop married Amy Bend, a New York socialite, and embarked on a life of travel and collecting. In the 1920s he purchased and later merged America's two major auction galleries. Bishop was also a bicyclist, motorist, balloonist, and owner of a chain of hotels in the Sahara and the Ritz Hotel in Paris. He built a magnificent house in the Berkshires and maintained a townhouse in Manhattan at 15 East Sixty-seventh Street, both filled with treasures accumulated over the years.

Bishop was an insatiable buyer of rare books, fine prints, and works of art, both privately and at auction, and eventually his collection was quite large. After Bishop's death his works of art and prints were sold by the American Art Association–Anderson Galleries. His books were also sold by the firm, but not until 1938, just after the company's managers, Hiram Parke and Otto Bernet, left to found their own firm. Mrs. Bishop's direction of her late husband's conglomerate brought about their departure and the eventual demise of the older organization in 1939.

Carved walnut cassone. Rome, sixteenth century. Height 31″. Columbus Museum of Fine Art, Columbus, Ohio. Bequest of Frederick W. Schumacher. Lot 651 in the C. F. Bishop sale at the American Art Association–Anderson Galleries on November 21–23, 1935. The catalogue entry noted that the sculptural quality of the chest was inspired by Roman sarcophagi of antiquity. Its price at the sale was $1,400.

1936

John Trumbull. *Giuseppe Ceracchi.* c. 1792. Oil on wood, 3¾ x 3¼". The Metropolitan Museum of Art, New York. Morris K. Jesup Fund, 1936. Lot 226 in a sale held at the Robert W. De Forest house at 7 Washington Square North, New York City, by the American Art Association–Anderson Galleries on January 29–30, 1936. The price was $900.

Few works of art invoke as many significant names in the artistic history of the United States as does this miniature. The artist, John Trumbull (1756–1843), soldier, diplomat, and painter, has here admirably captured the likeness of Giuseppe Ceracchi (1751–1802), an Italian sculptor who came to the United States in 1790 seeking a commission for a heroic marble statue of Liberty but who had to be content with doing a few portrait busts. On his return to Europe he became involved in a plot against Napoleon and was executed. An early owner of the miniature was Samuel Putnam Avery, art dealer, book collector, and benefactor of Columbia University's Avery Library. Its next owner was John Taylor Johnston, a New York collector and a founder of the Metropolitan Museum of Art. It was then owned by Mr. and Mrs. Robert W. De Forest, descendants of an old New York family, who lived in that still-preserved enclave of Knickerbocker society Washington Square. Today it is in the Metropolitan Museum.

Among the year's highlights were sales from the collections of Marsden J. Perry and Henry Graves, Jr. Perry (1850–1935), an entrepreneur of New England origins, was for some years a business associate of Richard A. Canfield (1855–1914), professional gambler and man-about-town, whose casino at Saratoga, New York, attracted the cream of society, and whose collection of paintings by his friend J. A. M. Whistler was legendary. Canfield was a charter member of the Walpole Society, founded in 1910 by the leading collectors of New York. Perry, Canfield, and a third associate, C. L. Pendleton (a benefactor of the Rhode Island School of Design Museum), were pioneer collectors of the decorative arts of the eighteenth century.

Perry acquired Canfield's furniture collection and sold some of it at an auction at the American Art Association in 1916. After Perry's death, the splendid English furniture, Chinese porcelains, and early silver from his house in Providence, Rhode Island, were acquired at his sale by collectors of a new generation, some perhaps not even old enough to remember Richard Canfield, the man responsible for starting Perry in collecting many years before.

The Henry Graves collection of fine prints was one of the most distinguished to appear at auction in America. Like so many sales of rare books and prints in those days, it was an evening affair, many of the bidders dressing for the occasion in dinner jackets. Old Master print sales in the 1920s and 1930s aroused the same kind of excitement that a major auction of modern paintings would in the 1980s.

The Graves catalogue contained 115 lots, arranged chronologically beginning with Dürer. Featured were the works of Frank Weston Benson, Rembrandt, Whistler, and James McBey, among other well-known printmakers.

Dürer's *Adam and Eve* fetched the high price of the evening; Rembrandt's etching *Christ Healing the Sick* (the so-called Hundred Guilder Print) $2,500 less, at $7,500.

In those days, the same auction-house department handled both books and prints, and the sales attracted many of the same collectors. This remained the case until the 1960s, when interest in prints skyrocketed. At that time Parke-Bernet in New York created a separate graphics department, which organized specialized sales of its own.

Albrecht Dürer. *Adam and Eve*. 1504. Engraving, first state of the finished plate, with small margins, 9⅞ x 7¾″. Lot 9 in the sale of the collection of Henry Graves, Jr., "Masterpieces of Engraving and Etching," on April 3, 1936, at the American Art Association–Anderson Galleries. The price fetched by this extraordinarily "brilliant proof in perfect state of preservation" was $10,000.

Adam and Eve was the engraving that brought Dürer's artistic powers to the attention of Europe's cognoscenti, and this particular example, on paper with a bull's-head watermark, can be traced back to the collection of Abraham Ortelius in the sixteenth century. The owner before Graves was Franz von Hagens, whose prints were auctioned in Leipzig in 1927.

Chippendale carved mahogany and French needlepoint armorial armchair. English, mid-eighteenth century. Height 51″. The Metropolitan Museum of Art, New York. Gift of Irwin Untermyer, 1964. One of a pair of ornate armchairs sold as lot 267 in the Marsden J. Perry collection sale on April 3–4, 1936, at the American Art Association–Anderson Galleries. The price for the pair was $1,550.

Chairs such as this presented many problems to early students of the furniture produced in Great Britain and her colonies during the eighteenth century. At various times experts have pronounced them to be English or Irish or American, only to have their views refuted by newer authorities and fresh research. At the Perry sale, the catalogue described this example as "English or Irish." It is now thought to be definitely English, and the armorial carving on the cresting has been identified as that of the marquess of Abergavenny. The prototype of this tour de force of furniture design is found in Chippendale's *Gentleman & Cabinet Maker's Director,* where it is called a "French chair."

1937

Neville Chamberlain, the British prime minister, attempts to achieve peace in Europe through conciliatory measures and appeasement of Germany.

Pablo Picasso paints *Guernica,* protesting the bombing of the Basque city during the Spanish Civil War.

Silver Monteith bowl, by John Coney. Boston, Massachusetts, c. 1710. Height 8⅝". Yale University Art Gallery, New Haven, Connecticut. The Mabel Brady Garvan Collection. Sold at the American Art Association–Anderson Galleries by George C. Gebelein of Boston at a special one-lot auction held on April 3, 1937, in conjunction with the Herbert Lawton collection sale of American furniture, portraits, and decorative objects. It brought $30,000.

One of the most important and splendid pieces of baroque American Colonial silver, this wine-glass cooler closely follows in style bowls produced in England from about 1690 to about 1710, except that English examples usually have removable rims. Wine glasses were suspended from the notched rim into the bowl, which held iced water. John Coney (1655–1722) made the bowl for John Colman, a prominent Boston merchant, whose arms are engraved inside, and in whose family it descended until the mid-nineteenth century.

John Sloan. *McSorley's Back Room*. 1916. Etching, 5¼ x 7". Private collection.

An example of this etching, and another etching also by Sloan, were sold together as lot 156 in the Cornelius J. Sullivan sale of furniture, paintings, prints, and other objects, held on April 29–30, 1937, at the American Art Association–Anderson Galleries. The lot fetched $25.

So sought-after have Sloan's prints of New York become in recent years that their prices have risen dramatically. The illustrated example was sold in New York at Sotheby Parke Bernet in February 1981 for $880*.

American Indian woven basket. Chemehueve tribe, Arizona. Height 11¾". Private collection.

Similar baskets were sold on October 29–30, 1937, in the auction of the Mr. and Mrs. Charles Baisley collection, titled "Art of the American Indian," at the American Art Association–Anderson Galleries. At that time, such a basket would have brought betweeen $5 and $65. The illustrated example, photographed for a Sotheby Parke Bernet sale in 1982, brought $12,100*. American Indian art auctions, held infrequently before the 1970s, have become regular features of the auction room in the past fifteen years.

John Singleton Copley. *Elizabeth Ross*. c. 1767. Oil on canvas, 50 x 40". Museum of Fine Arts, Boston, Massachusetts. M. and M. Karolik Collection of Eighteenth-Century American Arts. Lot 347 in the sale of the collection of Herbert Lawton of Boston, held at the American Art Association–Anderson Galleries on April 3, 1937, brought $5,000.

John Singleton Copley (1738–1815) painted this engaging likeness shortly before his masterpiece, *Paul Revere,* also in the Boston Museum. The sitter's pose in this picture is derived from an engraving of 1762 after a portrait by Sir Joshua Reynolds. The practice of using contemporary English prints after portraits by the most fashionable European painters of the day was widespread among the early artists of the British colonies in America, most of whom were self-taught.

Elizabeth Ross was born in Portland, Maine, in 1751. She married a British officer, Colonel Tyng, in 1769 and was forced to flee the Colonies to Canada with other Loyalists in 1783. She later returned to Maine, where she died in 1831.

1938

Thornton Wilder's play about rural New England life, *Our Town*, is published.

Orson Welles's radio play *Invasion from Mars* causes panic when many listeners believe it to be a report of an actual attack.

Henry Alken. *The Twenty-four Starters of the Derby Stakes.* c. 1842. Oil on canvas, 15½ x 24¼". Lot 1392 in the auction of the collection of Mary T. Carlisle of East Islip, Long Island, conducted by Parke-Bernet Galleries, Inc., at 742 Fifth Avenue (on the northwest corner of Fifty-seventh Street) on January 11–15, 1938. Parke and Bernet and their staff had left the American Art Association–Anderson Galleries in the fall of 1937. The first auction conducted by the new firm was the dispersal of the Carlisle collection of furniture, pictures, silver, and rugs. The event was considered a great success and a good omen for the future.

Henry Alken (1785–1851) is among the best known of the British sporting artists whose paintings and prints of hunting, shooting, and racing scenes have been perennial favorites among the American—as well as the British—upper classes.

The 1842 Derby was won by Colonel Anson's horse Attila, which was also the winner of the Champagne Stakes at Doncaster and the Clearwell Stakes at Newmarket in the same year.

In 1938 the picture, erroneously catalogued as *The Start for the Epsom Derby,* brought $1,350. In 1974, when it was sold as part of the Jack Dick collection of sporting paintings at Sotheby's, London, it brought $27,600.

1939

World War II begins after Germany invades Poland.

James Joyce's *Finnegans Wake* and John Steinbeck's *The Grapes of Wrath* are published.

King George VI and Queen Elizabeth visit the United States, the first British sovereigns to do so.

The sale of an unusually fine and varied group of modern paintings, drawings, sculptures, and prints from the estate of Mrs. Cornelius J. Sullivan attracted a standing-room-only crowd on the evenings of December 6 and 7. Not only did the objects stimulate competition but the arena was once again the building at 30 East Fifty-seventh Street. The American Art Association–Anderson Galleries had become defunct, and Parke, Bernet, and their staff were now back in the familiar salesroom where so many great auctions had taken place over the years.

Mrs. Sullivan was an active leader in the movement to show the newer trends in art in New York. Together with Mrs. John D. Rockefeller and Miss Lillie P. Bliss, she played an important role in founding the Museum of Modern Art. Naturally, the auction attracted crowds of Mrs. Sullivan's friends and admirers, who bid on the Picassos and Rouaults, the Dufys and Derains. Van Gogh's *Portrait of Mademoiselle Ravoux* brought $19,000, and Cézanne's *Portrait of Madame Cézanne* went for $27,500, the high price of the sale and the highest price of the season.

The purchaser of lot 184 in the Mrs. Cornelius J. Sullivan sale, accompanied by friends and chauffeur, in the elevator hall of the Parke-Bernet building at 30 East Fifty-seventh Street. Her purchase, seen leaning against a wall, was Camille Pissarro's gouache painting of 1885 titled *Marketplace at Pontoise,* which she bought for $850.

Auction-goers, some in formal attire, leaving Parke-Bernet Galleries after the Mrs. Cornelius J. Sullivan sale, December 6–7, 1939.

Three-color glazed pottery quatrefoil dish. Chinese, Liao Dynasty (947–1125). Length 12″. Private collection. Lot 589 in the William H. Whittredge collection, sold at Parke-Bernet Galleries on November 18, 1939, for $25. In February 1973 the dish was resold at Sotheby Parke Bernet, New York, for $34,000.

In the 1939 catalogue the piece was described as Tang Dynasty (618–907). Such early wares have achieved popularity and high prices only in recent years.

Hilaire Germaine Edgar Degas. *Standing Horse*. Bronze, length 15″. Acquavella Galleries, New York. Lot 150 in the auction of modern art from the estate of Mrs. Cornelius J. Sullivan, Parke-Bernet Galleries, December 6–7, 1939, brought $475. When this same bronze was sold again at Sotheby Parke Bernet, New York, in 1981, its price was $107,250*.

The wax sculptures of Degas cast in bronze after his death by Adrien Hébrard were limited to twenty sets intended for sale, marked with the letters A to T, plus a few other sets for Degas's heirs, the caster, the founder, and so forth. The "A" set, formerly in the collection of Mrs. H. O. Havemeyer, is now in the Metropolitan Museum of Art. Mrs. Sullivan owned nine examples from the "B" set, of which this was model number 38 *(Cheval Arrêté)*.

1940

Torso of a Satyr. Roman, first–second century A.D., after a Greek prototype of fourth century B.C. Marble, height 44″. Columbus Museum of Art, Columbus, Ohio. Howald Fund Purchase. Lot 119 in the auction of the Samuel Untermyer collection of paintings, tapestries, antiquities, and textiles, Parke-Bernet Galleries, May 10–11, 1940, brought $375.

When in 1877 John Ruskin, England's most influential critic, reviewed the inaugural exhibition at London's Grosvenor Gallery, he was, to put it mildly, exasperated. He was exasperated most of all with a picture titled *Nocturne in Black and Gold* and wrote of it: "For Mr. Whistler's sake, no less than for the protection of the purchaser, the Grosvenor Gallery ought not to have admitted works into the gallery in which the ill-educated conceit of the artist so nearly approached the aspect of imposture. I have seen and heard much of cockney impudence before now, but never expected to hear a coxcomb ask two hundred guineas for flinging a pot of paint in the public's face."

Mr. James A. M. Whistler—Massachusetts-born, a West Point dropout, trained in Paris, the toast of London's smart set—was as offended by Ruskin's words as the critic had been by his paintings. Accordingly, he filed suit for libel, asking £1,000 in damages.

By the time the trial took place sixteen months later, notoriety had caused Whistler's sales to drop off, and his flippant replies to the attorney general's questions at the trial did not help his case. He won, but lost; awarded one farthing in damages, he had to pay court costs, and this Pyrrhic victory put Whistler in financial straits so severe he had to auction his Chinese blue-and-white porcelain at Sotheby's, London, in February 1880.

Little more than a decade later, the tide had turned: the once unassailable Ruskin, plagued by nervous disorders, had seen his influence decline, and Whistler's exhibition at London's Goupil Gallery was a triumph. Best of all, perhaps, a noted American attorney, Samuel Untermyer of New York, purchased the notorious painting of falling rockets for eight hundred guineas (the equivalent of "four pots of paint," as Whistler gleefully pointed out).

Today *Nocturne in Black and Gold* hangs in the Detroit Institute of Arts, an "artistic arrangement" that in little more than a century has become an important monument of art history and contemporary taste rather than an example of a coxcomb's impudence.

The man to whom the *Nocturne* belonged, Samuel Untermyer (1858–1940), was a Virginian who became senior partner in a major New York law firm. He was active in corporate mergers and in antitrust matters, and while he was counsel for New York City's Transit Commission he managed to preserve the five-cent fare.

After the auction of his pictures and other works of art—which included examples by Cranach, Corot, Monet, and Gainsborough—two other sales were held to dispose of the contents of the Untermyer house, "Greystone," on the Hudson River at Yonkers, New York. Over a thousand lots of furniture and garden appointments and rare orchids, bougainvilleas, dieffenbachias, and streptocarpuses from the Untermyer greenhouses were all sold in situ.

Opposite: James Abbott McNeill Whistler. *Nocturne in Black and Gold: The Falling Rocket.* c. 1875. Oil on panel, 24¾ x 18⅜″. The Detroit Institute of Arts, Detroit, Michigan. Gift of Dexter M. Ferry, Jr. Lot 29 in the Samuel Untermyer collection auction at Parke-Bernet Galleries on May 10–11, 1940, fetched $7,000.

One of the most talked-about paintings in the annals of modern art, *Nocturne in Black and Gold* created only a minor sensation when it appeared at auction for the first (and only) time, at the Untermyer sale.

1941

United States declares war on Japan; Germany and Italy declare war on the United States.

Henry Moore executes a series of drawings inspired by the subway shelters and the air raids in London.

Carved agate vase (Rubens Vase). Roman, c. fourth century A.D. Height 7½". Walters Art Gallery, Baltimore, Maryland. Lot 1316 in the sale of Mrs. Henry Walters's art collection at Parke-Bernet Galleries, April 23–26, 1941. The price: $4,500.

According to art historian Michael Jaffe, the great Flemish painter-diplomat Sir Peter Paul Rubens bought this choice piece at the St. Germain fair in Paris in 1619. Later, in 1882, it appeared at the Hamilton Palace sales in London, and in 1925 it entered the famous collection of Sir Francis Cook, Bart.

One of the greatest of all American collectors was William T. Walters of Baltimore, who died in 1894 and left to his son, Henry Walters (1848–1931), a large and splendid group of paintings and other art objects. Henry, also a connoisseur and collector, presented the city of Baltimore with his treasures and a new museum to house them, the Walters Art Gallery.

Henry Walters's widow possessed an impressive collection of French decorative art. More than 1,400 lots of the finest jewels, paintings, carpets, tapestries, sculpture, porcelain, and furniture were offered at public auction in 1941, but due to the uncertainty of the times prices were depressed.

Louis XV tulipwood and fruitwood marquetry "bonheur du jour," attributed to Charles Topino. French, eighteenth century. Height 35¾″. Private collection. Lot 697 in the Mrs. Henry Walters sale at Parke-Bernet Galleries on April 23–26, 1941, sold for $2,900.

This lady's writing desk later entered the collection of Bernice Chrysler Garbisch and was included in her estate sale on May 17, 1980, as lot 318, at which time it brought $16,500*.

Charles Topino, who was admitted to the guild of master *ébénistes,* or cabinetmakers, in 1773, specialized in small tables and writing desks of this kind, featuring marquetry panels representing vases, utensils, and art objects in the Chinese taste. No attribution to Topino was made in the 1941 catalogue.

William Blake. *The Great Red Dragon and the
Woman Clothed with the Sun*. c. 1805–10. Watercolor, 15¾ x 12¾″. National Gallery of Art,
Washington, D.C. Rosenwald Collection. Lot
118 in the sale of the A. Edward Newton collection (Part I: A–D), Parke-Bernet Galleries, April
16–18, 1941, brought $10,000—the highest price
of the entire auction. Newton was a well-liked
and highly respected bibliophile and collector.
More than twenty-two watercolors by William
Blake were included in his sale.

Blake (1757–1827), the most enigmatic and
mystical figure in British art, painted more than
135 illustrations in tempera and watercolor of
biblical themes for his patron, Thomas Butts, a
government functionary.

Butts's collection was sold by his son at
Sotheby's, London, in 1852, and many of the
Blakes at the sale are still untraced, although
some were exhibited in Boston in 1876 and
subsequently auctioned at the American Art
Association in 1901.

Carved oak press-cupboard. English or Welsh, c. 1680. Height 82″. The Metropolitan Museum of Art, New York. Gift of Irwin Untermyer, 1964. Lot 1132 in the sale of the collection of the late Mr. and Mrs. Charles E. F. McCann of New York and Oyster Bay, Parke-Bernet Galleries, November 17–21, 1942, brought $500.

In its size, its tripart structure, and its profuse ornamentation, this piece of furniture is most unusual. The McCann collection contained fine silver, bronzes, French decorative arts, and carpets as well as superb English furniture. McCann, an advertising genius and co-founder of his own agency, shared a passion for collecting with his partner, Alfred W. Erickson, whose own collection would be offered at Parke-Bernet in November 1961 (see page 174).

Jean-Auguste-Dominique Ingres. *Raphael and the Fornarina*. 1840. Oil on canvas, 13¾ x 10¾". Columbus Museum of Art, Columbus, Ohio. Bequest of Frederick W. Schumacher. Lot 276A in the sale of the collection of Esther Slater Kerrigan, January 8–10, 1942, at Parke-Bernet Galleries brought $2,200.

Ingres (1780–1867), most famous for his splendid portraits and sumptuous odalisques, painted several small genre scenes dealing with the lives of famous artists, in this instance, Raphael. Legend has it that Raphael's mistress was a baker's wife *(fornarina)*. Ingres treated the subject four times. This version of 1840 was dedicated to his architect friend Félix Duban.

Mrs. Kerrigan's collection was diverse, comprising paintings and drawings by Daumier, Sargent, and Boudin, as well as Old Masters, bronzes, and French furniture.

1943

United States troops invade Italy; siege of Leningrad ends after twenty-seven months.

Rodgers and Hammerstein's *Oklahoma* is produced on Broadway, revolutionizing American musical theater.

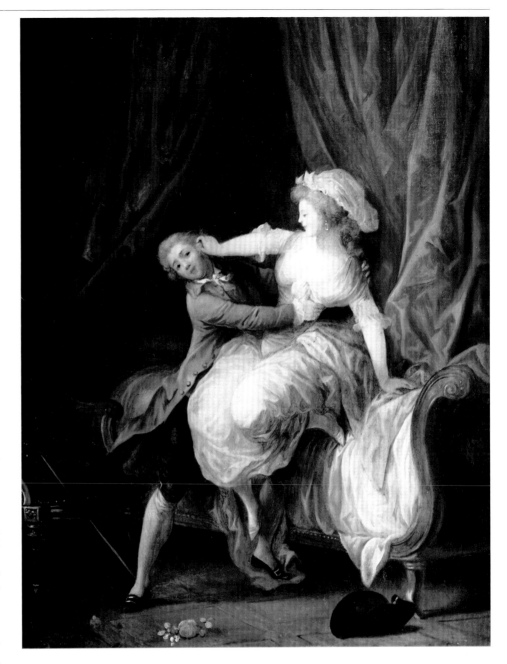

Jean-Frédéric Schall. *Useless Resistance*. Oil on panel, 12¾ x 9½". Private collection. Lot 365 in the auction of the collection of Condé Nast held at Parke-Bernet Galleries on January 9, 1943, brought $3,300. In 1975 Schall's picture was sold as part of the Charles E. Dunlop collection at Sotheby Parke Bernet, New York, when it brought $10,500.

Jean-Frédéric Schall (1753–1835) carried the traditions of Fragonard and Boucher into the post-Revolutionary period, often depicting couples in amorous, slightly "naughty" situations.

Condé Nast (1874–1942), whose publishing empire included *Vogue, House and Garden,* and *Vanity Fair,* and who was renowned for his lavish hospitality, had a huge apartment at 1040 Park Avenue, New York, the contents of which were sold after his death.

Frank Crowninshield, who was Condé Nast's chief lieutenant and the genius behind *Vanity Fair,* wrote the preface to the catalogue. The following October, Crowninshield's own superb collection of modern art was sold at Parke-Berret Galleries. Lionello Venturi, the noted art historian, pointed out in his foreword to the Crowninshield catalogue that the collector had helped to publicize the 1913 Armory Show, had served as the first secretary of the Museum of Modern Art, and had continually championed the best in contemporary artistic movements. Among the highest prices of the sale was $4,800—paid for Picasso's 1909 portrait of Georges Braque.

1944

Allied invasion of Normandy begins on D-Day.

Colette's controversial and popular *Gigi* is published.

Philippe de Champaigne. *Charles II, King of England*. 1653. Oil on canvas, 49½ x 39¼". The Cleveland Museum of Art, Cleveland, Ohio. Purchased from the Elisabeth Severance Prentiss Fund. Lot 85 in the sale of the collection of Stanley Mortimer of New York at Parke-Bernet Galleries on December 2, 1944, was bought by Joseph Duveen for $1,900.

Only when the picture was cleaned in 1958 did the date 1653 appear; thus, we now know the canvas was painted while the king was in exile during Oliver Cromwell's Commonwealth. Charles spent most of the time at the Château of Saint Germain, near Paris, as would his son James II, who died there in exile in 1701. The cliffs and port of Dover are visible in the left background, indicative of Charles's hopes of returning to England—which he did in 1660.

Stanley Mortimer's collection was a relatively small but extremely fine group of Old Masters, Renaissance bronzes, stained glass, and furniture, reminiscent of the taste of the 1920s.

Russian gold, mother-of-pearl, and enamel miniature sedan chair, designed by Peter Karl Fabergé, executed under the direction of workmaster Mikhail Perchin. St. Petersburg, c. 1900. Height 3¾″. The Forbes Magazine Collection, New York. Lot 430 in the sale of furniture and *objets d'art* from the estate of J. P. Morgan on January 6–7, 1944, at Parke-Bernet Galleries. It sold for $1,800.

Exquisite objects by Fabergé (1846–1920) are often in the Louis XVI taste, much favored by the czars Alexander III and Nicholas II and their courtiers. *Forbes* magazine's superb collection of Fabergé has done much to focus public attention on the delightful works of art produced in the great jeweler's workshops during the last years of the Romanov Dynasty.

1945

Japan surrenders following the atomic bombing of Hiroshima and Nagasaki.

President Franklin D. Roosevelt dies, succeeded by Harry S. Truman.

Baron Hendrik Leys. *The Education of Charles V.* 1861. Oil on panel, 36½ x 46″. Private collection. Lot 172 in the Vanderbilt sale brought $1,350. When it was sold in New York at Sotheby Parke Bernet in 1979, its price was $38,500*.

Baron Leys (1815–1869) was the foremost Belgian painter of his day, and his scenes of medieval and Renaissance life were extremely popular. Alma-Tadema was one of his pupils.

The auction of "distinguished Barbizon and genre paintings" from the collections of Cornelius Vanderbilt and William H. Vanderbilt, sold by order of Mrs. Cornelius Vanderbilt at Parke-Bernet Galleries in the spring, provides us with a vivid reminder of the rise, fall, and rise again to favor of some of the artists of the late nineteenth century. J.-F. Millet, whose *Angelus* had been the most expensive picture sold at auction in the nineteenth century, fared better than many of his contemporaries at sales in the early twentieth century—a pattern that has persisted until the present time, when extraordinarily high prices have been paid for both Millet's paintings and his drawings. Today's buyers are often Japanese millionaires, who appear to share the aesthetic preferences as well as the business acumen of nineteenth-century American tycoons.

At the Vanderbilt sale, prices for Corot, Daubigny, and Théodore Rousseau were only a fraction of what they would have been forty years earlier (or would be again in the 1980s). But lowest of all were the prices for the most celebrated "storytelling" painters of their day.

Sir Lawrence Alma-Tadema's *Sculpture Gallery* and *Picture Gallery* brought $850 and $1,000, respectively. *Entrance to a Roman Theatre,* which had been written about and engraved in 1879 for the book *Art Treasures of America,* sold for $1,300.

J.-G. Vibert, one of the shining stars of the Mary Jane Morgan sale of 1886, was represented by *Committee on Moral Books,* a depiction of a prelate and a friar gleefully reading forbidden tomes before throwing them into the flames; it went for $2,700. And J.-L. Gérôme's *Reception of the Prince de Condé by Louis XIV,* a canvas measuring 38 x 55 inches, also featured in *Art Treasures of America,* brought only $5,100.

How the mighty had fallen, thanks to a combination of Depression, war, and tastes that rejected academic painting as not worthy of consideration! Many of these once famous artists would, for all intents and purposes, cease to be mentioned except in the pages of auction catalogues. Not until modern art had reached what many saw as a dead end in the late 1960s was there a revival of interest in the Salon paintings our great-grandparents loved.

Jean-François Millet. *The Sower.* 1850. Oil on canvas, 39¾ x 31¾″. Lot 58 in the sale of the William H. Vanderbilt collection held at Parke-Bernet Galleries on April 18–19, 1945. *The Sower* brought $26,000, the second highest price of the sale; Millet's *Peasant Woman with Buckets* fetched $4,000 more.

In 1977 this picture was resold at Sotheby Parke Bernet in New York and then brought $300,000.

1946

War trials are held in Nuremberg, Germany.

Winston Churchill makes his famous "Iron Curtain" speech in Fulton, Missouri.

Many of the collections formed during the heady days of the 1920s and in the early 1930s were now being dispersed—and bargains were to be had: Gilbert Stuart portraits sold by the descendants of John Quincy Adams fetched $3,000 and less. The contents of actress Marion Davies's palatial home in Santa Monica, California—English and American furniture, silver, and porcelains—brought less than $200,000 for 429 lots.

The buying power of the British and Continental dealers and collectors had been obliterated by war and currency controls, and for the moment, at least, Americans had other things on their minds and other priorities in their spending. In the late 1940s many artistic reputations of the prewar era, Louis Comfort Tiffany's among them, reached a nadir. It was a period of transition to a new postwar age, and another ten years would pass before the situation changed.

49.

and her eyes immediately met those of a large blue caterpillar, which was sitting with its arms folded, quietly smoking a long hookah, and taking not the least notice of her or of anything else.

For some time they looked at each other in silence: at last the caterpillar took the hookah out of its mouth, and languidly addressed her.

"Who are you?" said the caterpillar.

This was not an encouraging opening for a conversation: Alice replied rather shyly, "I— I hardly know, sir, just at present— at least I know who I _was_ when I got up this morning, but I think I must have been changed several times since that."

"What do you mean by that?" said the caterpillar, "explain yourself!"

"I ca'n't explain _myself_, I'm afraid, sir,"

Lewis Carroll's autograph manuscript of *Alice's Adventures in Wonderland* (then entitled *Alice's Adventures under Ground*), of about 1864. Ninety pages, including "illuminated" title page and dedication leaf, fourteen full-page drawings, and twenty-three text illustrations by the author. The British Library, London. Illustrated here is a page of text. Lot 51 in the sale of the library and collection (Part I) of Eldridge R. Johnson of Moorestown, New Jersey, on April 3–4, 1946, at Parke-Bernet Galleries, this original manuscript of Carroll's classic brought $50,000. It was presented to the Library of Congress in Washington by the noted book dealer Dr. A.S.W. Rosenbach (1876–1952) and a group of collectors, to be given to the British Library, the appropriate home for the famous book.

The first printed edition of *Alice* (1865) had the famous Sir John Tenniel illustrations, which followed rather closely Carroll's own drawings. A facsimile edition of the manuscript was issued in 1886, and Mrs. Hargreaves (née Alice Liddell, the model for the book's chief character), sold the original at Sotheby's in London on April 3, 1928. Dr. Rosenbach purchased it at that sale for £15,400, then the highest price ever paid at auction in England for a book. It then entered the collection of Eldridge R. Johnson.

Lewis Carroll was the pseudonym of the Reverend Charles L. Dodgson (1832–1898), whose many children's stories, developed out of tales he told to Alice Liddell and her friends, have made him one of the best-known figures in English literature.

Pair of Tiffany covered urns. Enamel on copper, height 11″. Private collection. Lot 314 in the auction of the contents of Laurelton Hall, Cold Spring Harbor, New York, the home of Louis Comfort Tiffany and the foundation he established. The sale took place September 24–28, 1946, at Parke-Bernet Galleries. The pair of vases brought $210.

When this same pair was reoffered as part of the Riseman collection of Tiffany pieces at Sotheby Parke Bernet, New York, on October 30, 1975, they fetched $14,000.

Son of the founder of the firm of Tiffany &

Company, Louis Comfort Tiffany (1848–1933) was a painter, designer, decorator, and art patron. His decorating firm eventually became Tiffany Studios, and here were crafted the favrile-glass and stained-glass creations that eventually brought him worldwide fame and made his name a household word. The foundation he established in 1919 was meant to occupy Laurelton Hall forever, but financial difficulties made it necessary to close the building and sell the collections. Since the mid-1960s, Tiffany's works have again become highly regarded by collectors, and price rises continue unabated.

1947

"Cold War" is underway; Truman Doctrine is promulgated; Soviets denounce the United States as warmongers.

Britain's former colony is divided into two independent nations, India and Pakistan.

Tennessee Williams's *A Streetcar Named Desire* is published.

The Whole Booke of Psalmes Faithfully Translated into English Metre, commonly known as the Bay Psalm Book, was the first book printed in the English colonies of North America, by Stephen Daye and his son, Matthew, at Cambridge, Massachusetts in 1640. Of an edition of approximately 1,700 copies only eleven have survived, and the copy sold at Parke-Bernet in 1947 can be traced back to the Reverend Thomas Prince, minister of Boston's Old South Church in the eighteenth century. Prince owned five copies, and one of them found its way into the library of the Massachusetts collector Edward Crowninshield, whose books were eventually bought by a London dealer, Henry Stevens; he, in turn, sold the Bay Psalm Book to George Brinley of Hartford, Connecticut. When Brinley's library was sold at auction in 1879, Cornelius Vanderbilt acquired the Bay Psalm Book for $1,200. It later entered the Gertrude Vanderbilt Whitney Charitable Trust, administered by members of the Whitney family, who eventually decided to sell the book in order to raise funds for the Glen Cove Community Hospital.

At the auction John Fleming, then the assistant and later the successor to book dealer Dr. A.S.W. Rosenbach, represented a group of "friends of Yale," who were determined to secure the volume for the university's library. Bidding began at $30,000 and proceeded very slowly to $55,000. Then young Sonny Whitney started bidding for himself in $5,000 increments. Fleming kept bidding, too, beyond the amount actually pledged by the Yale contingent, up to and then past the auction record of $106,000 set in 1926 for Melk Abbey's Gutenberg Bible, and he eventually made the high bid of $151,000. The room was silent until the auctioneer's hammer finally banged down, and then the audience cheered.

Yale's benefactors had quite a struggle to raise the funds, almost double their original pledge. However, after a brief delay, the Bay Psalm Book was presented to the university's library.

Bay Psalm Book. Cambridge, Massachusetts, 1640. Beinecke Rare Book and Manuscript Library, New Haven, Connecticut. Sold at Parke-Bernet Galleries in a special one-lot auction on January 28, 1947, for $151,000. Illustrated is the title page.

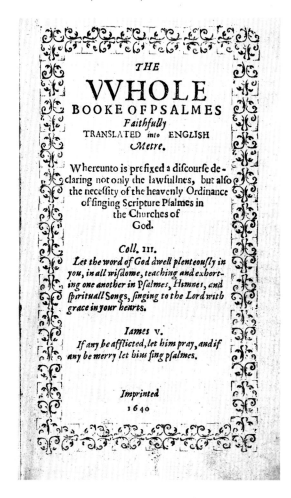

Elizabethan parcel-gilt silver ewer and basin, decorated with royal portraits and scenes from the Old Testament. London, 1567. Engraving possibly by Pieter Maas (mark: P over M); silversmith unknown (mark: L reversed). Height of ewer 13³⁄₁₆″; diameter of basin 19⁵⁄₈″. Museum of Fine Arts, Boston, Massachusetts. Theodora Wilbour Fund in memory of Charlotte Beebe Wilbour. Lot 466 in the auction of silver from the J. P. Morgan collection, sold at Parke-Bernet Galleries on October 31, 1947, brought $17,500.

The finely engraved medallions of British kings and Old Testament figures are all captioned in Latin, and the inscription around the dish refers to the cleansing of sins through the blood of Christ, perhaps suggesting a royal baptismal or other religious ceremonial use.

John Pierpont Morgan (1837–1913) built his family's already considerable fortune and prestige into one of the world's most formidable reserves of wealth and power. Morgan's business interests extended from finance to railroads, mines, steel, shipping, and insurance. His collection was virtually without peer in terms of quality and quantity, and it ranged from medieval manuscripts to Chinese porcelains. The Morgan Library and the Metropolitan Museum received the bulk of his collection, but a part remained with his son John Pierpont Morgan (1867–1943) and was sold after his death.

1948

Demand continued to remain low for many of the kinds of art and antiques that had been popular before the Depression and World War II. Despite the generally sluggish art and book market, Parke-Bernet Galleries in a daring move decided to shift its operations a mile further uptown, to new space in a specially designed building at Madison Avenue and Seventy-sixth Street. This was the second move uptown for the firm that had begun its life in 1883 on Madison Square.

Federal inlaid mahogany card table, by John Townsend. Newport, Rhode Island, 1794. Height 28¼". Mr. and Mrs. Stanley Stone collection. One of a pair of tables comprising lot 215 in a sale of American furniture belonging to Joseph Hirshhorn, held at Parke-Bernet Galleries on December 10, 1948. Price for the pair: $2,050. The tables had been included in the Flayderman sale of 1930, where they brought $5,600.

John Townsend (1732–1809) was a member of the Goddard-Townsend family of cabinet-makers, whose most famous productions were the blockfront pieces made before the Revolutionary War. These labeled card tables demonstrated how thoroughly a later generation had absorbed the newer, Neoclassical principles of refinement and utility in design.

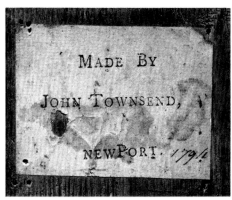

Grant Wood. *The Birthplace of Herbert Hoover.* 1931. Oil on masonite, 29⅝ x 39¾″. The Minneapolis Institute of Arts, the John R. Van Derlip Fund 81.105, and the Des Moines Art Center. Lot 31 in the auction of the collection of American furniture, silver, and paintings belonging to Mr. Ralph Blum of Beverly Hills, California, on November 6, 1948, at Parke-Bernet Galleries. The painting brought $6,500.

While Hoover was campaigning for election in 1932 and simultaneously trying to cope with the Depression and compete for votes with Franklin D. Roosevelt, some of Iowa's leading citizens commissioned the state's own Grant Wood (1892–1942) to paint the birthplace of the "Great Engineer" at West Branch. Their intent was to show the humble origins of the man, who was, they felt, wrongly perceived to be more concerned with protecting business than shielding workers from the effects of the Great Depression.

From Grant Wood's distinctive bird's-eye point of view, we see the house that was later added to the shed in which Hoover was born in 1874, as well as the Wapsinonac Creek, where he swam, and the neatly manicured surrounding grounds. A tiny Everyman figure points out the scene to the observer, in the tradition of early American paintings.

Hoover, neither amused nor impressed, rejected the painting. He also, of course, lost the election.

1949

North Atlantic Treaty Organization (NATO) is established.

Arthur Miller's play *Death of a Salesman* is published.

In the spring following the death of famed New York art dealer Joseph Brummer, his remarkable collection of art from many periods came on the market.

The number of superb objects that were formerly in Brummer's collection and are now in America's major museums is a tribute to the discerning eye of this extraordinary man. Egyptian sculpture, Byzantine ivories, Gothic statuary, pre-Columbian pottery, liturgical vessels and vestments of the Middle Ages, stained glass, Limoges enamels, and splendid architectural fragments were all included in the sale. There was even a sculptured stone rose window, which had formerly been in the collection of William Randolph Hearst. It brought $150. The wood pedestals from the Brummer Gallery at 110 East Fifty-eighth Street went for $2 each.

Joseph Brummer's interests had not been confined to antiques alone. He was advisor to John Quinn and helped to dispose of the Quinn collection after his friend's death in 1924. Although interest in modern art had increased greatly in the intervening years, price levels were still low in 1949. At the auction of the collection of noted film director Josef von Sternberg in November, for instance, a major Chagall painting of 1930 fetched $3,300; a Kokoschka oil of London Bridge brought $5,500; and the stunning Modigliani *Grand Nu* shown here sold for $12,500—the high price of the sale.

Parke-Bernet Galleries were now ensconced at 980 Madison Avenue, but the art market was still a sleeping giant and the area around Seventy-sixth Street remained quietly residential.

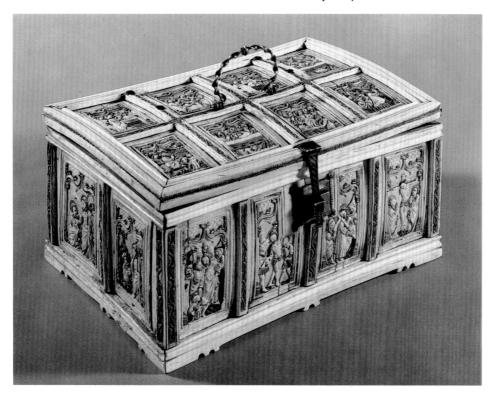

Gothic carved, polychromed, and parcel-gilt ivory casket. French, late fourteenth century. Length 12¼". Wadsworth Atheneum, Hartford, Connecticut. Gift of Mrs. Charles C. Cunningham. This was lot 697 in the sale of the Joseph Brummer collection on May 11–14, 1949, at Parke-Bernet Galleries. The price was $1,300.

Amedeo Modigliani. *Reclining Nude (Grand Nu)*. c. 1919. Oil on canvas, 28½ x 45⅞". The Museum of Modern Art, New York. Mrs. Simon Guggenheim Fund. Lot 92 in the auction of Josef von Sternberg's collection at Parke-Bernet Galleries on November 22, 1949, fetched $12,500.

Born in Vienna, von Sternberg has always been considered one of the great names of the cinema. He was one of many European emigrés who helped promote and popularize the collecting of modern art.

Together with Titian, Velázquez, Boucher, and Ingres, Modigliani (1884–1920) must be ranked as one of the great masters of the female nude in painting. Often depicted in languid, horizontal poses, Modigliani's nudes combined voluptuousness and cool detachment in a striking manner that is thoroughly modern and uniquely Modigliani's.

Silver vitrine set with jewels, designed by Carl Otto Czeschka. Vienna (Wiener Werkstätte), 1903. Height 5′4½″. Lot 1045, auction of the collection of Mrs. Jerome Stonborough, Parke-Bernet Galleries, March 4, 1949. The price: $1,075.

In 1949 the productions of Josef Hoffmann's early twentieth-century craft studios in Vienna were out of favor with collectors; even such a special and costly piece as this vitrine, made for the famous Kunstschau of 1908 and immediately acquired by the Viennese patron of modern art Herr von Wittgenstein, went for very little. Only in the 1970s did the superb design and crafsmanship of this Viennese arts-and-crafts movement again come to be appreciated. Hoffmann (1870–1956) designed furniture, glass, and jewelry as well as works in metal, and he was the presiding genius of the Wiener Werkstätte's efforts. When this vitrine was resold at Sotheby Parke Bernet, New York, in December 1983, it brought $275,000*.

1950

President Truman sends United States troops to Korea.

Jackson Pollock's *Lavender Mist,* an early masterpiece of "drip," or "action," painting, is completed.

Charles Schulz's comic strip "Peanuts" makes a debut.

Constantin Brancusi. *Mademoiselle Pogany.* c. 1913. Bronze, height 17¼″. Private collection. As *Head of a Woman,* this sculpture was lot 37 in the sale of the second part of the collection of Walter P. Chrysler, Jr., on February 16, 1950, at Parke-Bernet Galleries. It brought $1,700. A Matisse painting of 1910 fetched the highest price of the evening: $5,500.

Margit Pogany was a Hungarian painter who met Brancusi (1876–1957) when she was studying art in Paris. She posed for the sculptor in 1910 and 1911, but her marble "portrait" was not finished until 1912, and the bronze version was not completed until about 1913.

Brancusi, who arrived in Paris in 1904, first came to the attention of the American public in 1913, when a plaster cast of *Mademoiselle Pogany* was exhibited at the Armory Show.

1951

General Douglas MacArthur is relieved of his command in Korea by President Truman.

Peace conference in San Francisco officially ends the war with Japan.

J. D. Salinger's *Catcher in the Rye* is published.

Prices still remained stubbornly low compared to the heady days before the Depression and World War II. Shelley's own copy of his early poem *Queen Mab* (1813), which had fetched the large sum of $18,000 at the Jerome Kern book sale at the American Art Association–Anderson Galleries in 1929, brought only $8,000 in 1951. The purchaser at the Kern sale was a bookseller, Gabriel Wells, whose stock was sold at auction after his death in 1951.

A series of auctions were held this year at Parke-Bernet, at which the estate of William Randolph Hearst sold off many art objects collected years before by the nabob publisher and lord of San Simeon castle.

A cup attributed to Cellini, for which Hearst had paid more than $30,000 in London, sold in New York for a mere $10,500.

One of the highest prices fetched during the doldrum year of 1951 was $16,000, for a Goddard-Townsend blockfront kneehole desk with shell relief carvings, which was put on the block during the Norvin Green Americana sale on November 29–December 1.

It was definitely a buyer's market, and astute collectors had many fine offerings from which to choose.

Left: Simone Martini. *Male Saint with a Book.* Tempera on panel, gold ground, 8¼ x 8¾". Museum of Fine Arts, Boston, Massachusetts. Purchased, Charles Potter Kling Fund. Lot 305 in the collection sale of Carrie W. Meinhard at Parke-Bernet Galleries on May 4–5, 1951. It sold for $6,500.

This small panel, together with a similarly shaped painting in the City Museum and Art Gallery, Birmingham, England, probably made up part of the predella of an altarpiece. It has been dated by various authorities about 1315, 1320, 1325, and even later.

Opposite: Jean Baptiste Siméon Chardin. *Still Life: A Kitchen Table with Skate.* c. 1732. Oil on canvas, 16 x 13". Private collection. Lot 68 in a sale of Old Masters held at Parke-Bernet Galleries on March 14, 1951, brought $1,300. Two smaller Chardins sold for $750 and $450, respectively.

When the picture reappeared again at auction, at Sotheby's, New York, in 1983, the price was $110,000*.

Chardin (1699–1779) painted several replicas and variants of this composition; three of the best known are in the Wadsworth Atheneum, Hartford, Connecticut; the Norton Simon Museum, Pasadena, California; and the North Carolina Museum of Art, Raleigh. The latter, dated 1731, is titled *Rayfish and Basket of Onions.*

1952

Fashions in historical manuscripts and memorabilia come and go as in other fields of collecting, but Abraham Lincoln's position remains preeminent in the market for American manuscripts and what are known in the trade as "association items." Lincoln's compelling personality, his position of leadership during the tragic Civil War, his marvelous command of the English language, and his death by an assassin's bullet have all contributed to his continuing mystique and an ongoing demand for his letters, documents, and personal items.

The dispersal of the Oliver Barrett collection was the greatest Lincolniana sale ever held, and material from this auction is found today in virtually every major Lincoln collection, public or private.

By coincidence, the famous 1860 "First Portrait" of the beardless Lincoln was sold at auction in 1952 as well. The purchaser was the Cuban industrialist-diplomat Oscar B. Cintas, who presented the portrait to the Chicago Historical Society for their Lincoln Collection. Just three years earlier, Cintas had made auction history at Parke-Bernet Galleries by paying $54,000 for the splendid manuscript copy of Lincoln's Gettysburg Address shown below, which he donated to the White House.

At recent Sotheby Parke Bernet auctions, many important Lincoln letters have appeared, as well as a wealth of association material, such as Lincoln's opera glasses and top hat, sold in 1979 from the Roy P. Crocker collection.

Above: Autograph letter dated April 2, 1865, from Abraham Lincoln to Mary Todd Lincoln.

There were a number of fine Lincoln manuscripts in the Oliver Barrett collection. The letter illustrated above, not in the Barrett sale, probably the last written communication between Lincoln and his wife, was sent from City Point, Virginia, General Grant's headquarters, while the president was visiting the front lines just a few days before his assassination. In 1983 it brought $48,400* at Sotheby Parke Bernet in New York, the record high price for a Lincoln letter.

Below: Abraham Lincoln's Gettysburg Address. 1863. Three-page holograph manuscript on blue ruled paper, 10 x 8". The White House Collection, Washington, D.C. Sold on April 27, 1949, at Parke-Bernet Galleries.

This copy of Lincoln's most famous speech was made by the president himself in an effort to help raise funds for the Sanitary Commission. Lieutenant Colonel Alexander Bliss and author J. P. Kennedy had persuaded the most prominent writers of the day to donate original manuscripts to be printed in a special book, *Autograph Leaves of Our Country's Authors,* which would be put up for sale at the Sanitary Commission's fair in Baltimore in 1864. Few of the books were sold, but this manuscript remained in the Bliss family collection until 1949. The fact that it is the only signed, titled, and dated version of the five known drafts of Lincoln's great address, as well as the only copy ever offered for sale, accounts for the record price it fetched at the auction: $54,000.

Gold watch chain presented to Abraham Lincoln. c. 1861. Chicago Historical Society, 1952.74a. Lot 482 in the Oliver Barrett Lincolniana collection sale, held at Parke-Bernet Galleries on February 19–20, 1952. The price was $1,300.

This chain of California gold was presented to Lincoln by a committee of the Union Pacific and Central Pacific railroads when they visited the capital to urge the national government to help build the transcontinental line. After the president's death, the chain was given by Mrs. Lincoln to a nephew. It was later acquired by Oliver Barrett.

Thomas Hicks. *Abraham Lincoln*. 1860. Oil on canvas, 24½ x 19¼". Chicago Historical Society, 1959.212. Lot 677 in the Vernon S. Prentice collection sale,. held at Parke-Bernet on April 17–19, 1952. The price was $18,000.

A Chicago art dealer sent Thomas Hicks (1823–1890) to paint the first portrait of Abraham Lincoln, in Springfield, Illinois, where Lincoln had his law office, after his nomination as Republican candidate for the presidency in the campaign of 1860.

In 1940, when a descendant of the original owner, Mrs. Herbert Shipman, consigned this same portrait for sale at Parke-Bernet, the price was $11,000.

1953

Armistice ends hostilities in Korea.

Raoul Dufy, chief decorative painter of the School of Paris, dies, as does John Marin, one of the original Stieglitz group.

Edmund Hillary and Tenzing Norkay become the first men to climb Mount Everest.

The early 1950s witnessed the gradual development of what would eventually become a highly popular and dynamic collecting area: modern prints, especially those done in colors by the Impressionists, the Postimpressionists, and their younger colleagues.

Widening appreciation for modern French painting carried over into allied forms of expression, such as lithography, in which many of the same artists were involved.

Tastes had changed since the 1920s and 1930s, and many of the technically superb black-and-white etchings and engravings admired by an earlier generation were now relegated to portfolios, while colorful prints by Picasso, Bonnard, and Toulouse-Lautrec were framed and displayed on the wall.

After long years of being known and appreciated only by a small group of specialist-collectors, modern illustrated French books began to find a wider audience, too.

Often these modern prints, posters, and books were included as the opening lots in Parke-Bernet sales of modern paintings and sculpture during the 1950s.

Today, sales of modern prints are a staple of the auction market, and their heavily illustrated catalogues have become authoritative guides to this active collecting area.

Opposite: Henri de Toulouse-Lautrec. *Marcelle Lender en Buste.* 1895. Lithograph printed in colors, third state of three. 12¾ x 9½".
A lithograph by Toulouse-Lautrec of Madame Lender, a well-known actress and singer acclaimed for her appearances in Hervé's operetta *Chilpéric* in 1895, was lot 147 in a sale of modern art, which included prints, consigned by the Kleeman Galleries, on the evening of April 7, 1953. The price was $250. The illustrated example was sold at Sotheby Parke Bernet in New York in 1983 for $15,950*.

1954

"McCarthyism" period ends as Senator Joseph McCarthy is censured by the United States Senate.

Ernest Hemingway receives the Nobel Prize in Literature.

Graham Sutherland's portrait of Winston Churchill so offends the sitter that it is not shown.

The Katherine Deere Butterworth sale in October serves as a good barometer of the art market during the mid-1950s. Barbizon and other nineteenth-century paintings were still bringing far less than they had during the 1920s, but the market for certain Dutch masters of the seventeenth century was beginning to recover. Most obviously, the so-called Duveen Market for expensive British portraits had fallen resoundingly.

In the catalogue entry for Raeburn's portrait of Mrs. Robertson Williamson, the picture's long and distinguished provenance was duly noted. Two former owners had sold the picture at auction. The first, a descendant of the sitter, realized 22,300 guineas (more than $100,000) in 1911, when it was knocked down in London. In 1926 Mrs. Williamson's portrait made a second appearance, at Hampton & Sons, London, when Lord Michelham's collection was auctioned off on November 24. The price was £24,675 ($123,375) to Knoedler's, who then sold it to Andrew Mellon. But the high price of the auction (£77,000) was brought by Sir Thomas Lawrence's famous portrait *Pinkie,* now in the Henry Huntington Library and Art Gallery in San Marino, California.

Sir Henry Raeburn. *Portrait of Mrs. Robertson Williamson.* c. 1823. Oil on canvas, 58 x 46″. Columbus Museum of Art, Columbus, Ohio. Bequest of Frederick W. Schumacher. Lot 35 in the sale of Old Masters and later paintings from the collection of Katherine Deere Butterworth of Moline, Illinois, at Parke-Bernet Galleries on October 20, 1954. The price: $14,000.

Mrs. Williamson was the daughter of William Boyd Robertson; she married her cousin, David Robertson Williamson, afterward Lord Balgray. The painting was originally full-length but was cut down to the three-quarter-length format during the 1930s; the low price it fetched at the Butterworth sale may in part reflect its reduction in size.

Sir Henry Raeburn (1756–1823), called the Scottish Reynolds, had been one of the world's most expensive painters early in the twentieth century. His best portraits were still relatively expensive but, in actual amounts, much depressed.

Charles Willson Peale. *Benjamin and Eleanor Ridgely Laming*. 1788. Oil on canvas, 42 x 60¼". National Gallery of Art, Washington, D.C. Gift of Morris Shapiro, 1966. Lot 455 in the sale of the collection of the famous author, antiquarian, and scholar of American arts and crafts Luke Vincent Lockwood, of Greenwich, Connecticut, held at Parke-Bernet Galleries on May 13–15, 1954. The price was $16,000.

Lockwood had been one of the organizers of the 1929 Girl Scout Exhibition, where this portrait was prominently displayed.

Charles Coleman Sellers, in his definitive study of the life of Charles Willson Peale (1741–1827), observes that "the reclining pose with spyglass is Peale's solution to the problem of bringing a large husband and a small wife into a balanced and graceful composition." Benjamin Laming was a native of the West Indies who became a prosperous merchant in Baltimore, Maryland. The townscape in the background of the painting represents a view of that city.

Winston Churchill resigns and is succeeded as prime minister of Great Britain by Anthony Eden.

General Motors reports earnings of more than $1 billion—the first corporation to achieve this annual earnings figure.

In 1671 Johannis Nys (1671–1734) was baptized in the Dutch church in New York, to which city his family had emigrated from Holland a few years earlier. They and other Huguenot families had been forced by religious persecution to flee France and the Low Countries. The departure of so many talented and industrious Calvinist artisans was a great loss to Europe; however, these Huguenot craftsmen brought new skills and ideas to British and American silversmithing: Paul de Lamerie, one of England's foremost rococo silversmiths, was a Huguenot refugee, as were Paul Revere in Boston, and Cesar Ghiselin and Johannis Nys in Philadelphia.

In 1695, after having learned the silversmiths' art in New York, Nys moved to fast-growing Philadelphia (soon to be the second largest city in the British Empire, after London), and eventually he prospered there. He made the tankard illustrated here for James and Sarah Logan, prominent Philadelphians, and it descended in the Logan family until it was acquired by Maurice Brix, a respected collector of fine American silver.

American silver has been collected for a century now, but scholarship is still bringing to light new information and insights about the art and craft of silversmithing in the British colonies and the early United States. Since no guilds existed, the whole approach to marking and dating pieces was much more haphazard than the orderly system that had prevailed in England from very early times. Consequently, the facts about various smiths' work and their biographical data are still far from complete. Paul Revere is, of course, the best known of all these early artisans, thanks to his many other well-publicized activities at the time of the American Revolution.

Silver flat-top tankard, known as the Logan Tankard, by Johannis Nys. Philadelphia, c. 1720. Height 7¼″. Philadelphia Museum of Art, Philadelphia, Pennsylvania. Purchased. Lot 273 in the sale of important American silver collected by Maurice Brix of Philadelphia, auctioned at Parke-Bernet Galleries on October 19–20, 1955. The most expensive lot in the sale, this tankard brought $4,500.

Childe Hassam. *Church at Old Lyme*. 1906. Oil on canvas, 30⅛ x 25¼″. The Parrish Art Museum, Southampton, New York. Littlejohn Collection. Lot 86 in a sale of the paintings of various owners held at Parke-Bernet Galleries on May 11, 1955. The price achieved was $3,000.

Early in the century, a group of painters including Henry Ward Ranger, Guy Wiggins, and Willard Metcalf began spending summers in the quaint village of Old Lyme, at the mouth of the Connecticut River, in New London County, Connecticut. Childe Hassam (1859–1935), perhaps the best known and most prolific of all the American Impressionists, first visited Old Lyme in 1903, and he joined the members of this budding art colony for the next several summers.

The fine old Congregational Church on the village green was painted more than once by Hassam before he forsook Old Lyme for New Hampshire and—finally—East Hampton, Long Island, where he resided during the last years of his life.

1956

When *Staffa, Fingal's Cave* was first shown at the Royal Academy in 1832, it was praised by the critics. "All is unison in this fine picture... sublimity of vastness and solitude" were typical reactions. Even so, the picture remained unsold in 1847, when the American expatriate artist Charles Robert Leslie came to J. M. W. Turner's studio on a mission to buy one of his paintings for a most unusual collector.

James Lenox (1800–1880) was the only son of a Scottish merchant who had emigrated to New York City in 1784 and prospered mightily. When his father died in 1840, James Lenox—a Princeton-educated, strict Presbyterian, confirmed bachelor—inherited a vast fortune that included a large tract of vacant land on the northeast side of Manhattan Island. He sold most of it off in lots, except for a small portion of what is today the East Sixties and Seventies, still known as Lenox Hill. Where the Frick Collection stands today he built an imposing library with its own park. He had a picture gallery in his house at 53 Fifth Avenue and decided he wanted to have a painting by Turner to exhibit there. Accordingly, he commissioned Leslie to obtain one for him, and Turner is reported to have said to the artist:

Joseph Mallord William Turner. *Staffa, Fingal's Cave.* c. 1831–32. Oil on canvas, 35¾ x 47¾". Yale Center for British Art, New Haven, Connecticut. Paul Mellon Collection. Lot 39 in a sale of paintings held at Parke-Bernet on October 17, 1956. Consigned by the New York

Public Library, it brought $47,000.

In the summer of 1831, while Turner was touring Scotland, he embarked one August day on the steamer "Maid of Morven" for the island of Staffa in the Inner Hebrides to see the famous caverns, especially the one called Fingal's Cave.

A storm came up and, as Turner explained to the painting's first owner, "the sun getting toward the horizon, burst through the rain-cloud, angry... we were driven to shelter ... and did not get back [to port] before midnight."

"I have no picture to sell to your American friend. No. My pictures are not adapted to American tastes or American appreciation of Art." "Well, Mr. Turner," Leslie countered, "you are in this matter mistaken, I assure you, for I . . . am tolerably well acquainted with the art characteristics of that growing country. Besides, I well know Mr. Lenox and am sure a picture of yours could not find a better home on either side of the Atlantic. . . . Here is Mr. Lenox's letter and a draft for £800. . . . Pray select such a picture as will, in your own best judgment, do yourself the most credit in the Art-benighted country you decry."

Turner selected *Staffa;* it was sent off to Mr. Lenox in New York, and the new owner was at first put off by the "indistinct" quality of the work. When Turner heard this he said, "Indistinctness is my fault," and he wrote Lenox to explain the picture and how it came to be painted.

Lenox, a philanthropist cast in a heroic mold, founded the Presbyterian Hospital and Home, and left his library and collections to the people of New York. In 1893 these were incorporated into the New York Public Library. Included in this legacy were a Gutenberg Bible (bought at Sotheby's, London, for £500 in 1847), a folio edition of Shakespeare, Washington's Farewell Address, and this Turner, the first painting by the artist to arrive in America. In 1956 the New York Public Library decided to sell *Staffa, Fingal's Cave* at auction. It was purchased by a London dealer and then entered the collection of Viscount Astor (a descendant of the man whose library formed another part of the present New York Public Library).

Just a few years ago *Staffa, Fingal's Cave* was acquired by the Yale Center for British Art. It would be hard to think of a more appropriate final home for this painting with such a distinguished Anglo-American provenance.

The Lenox Library, at Fifth Avenue and Seventieth Street, New York. Designed for James Lenox by architect Richard Morris Hunt, it was built in 1870–75 and demolished in 1912. Seen at left, across Seventieth Street, is one of the many opulent mansions that lined Fifth Avenue.

The New York Public Library's main building, at Fifth Avenue and Forty-second Street, which incorporates the Astor Library, the Lenox Library, and the Tilden Trust. It was the third home of J. M. W. Turner's *Staffa, Fingal's Cave*.

1957

The year got off to a resounding start in January with the dispersal of the collection of Mrs. Sarah MacCadwell Manwaring Plant Hayward Rovensky. So vast was the extent of her possessions that Parke-Bernet's president, Leslie Hyam, confessed in the foreword to the catalogue: "It is a rare experience to sit, pen in hand, and ask oneself how [the collection] can possibly be epitomized for the reader." He concluded, after mentioning some of the highlights of the late owner's New York mansion and her Newport house, "Here was someone who believed with great sincerity that the social order was immutably secure; that the meaning of wealth, as with the merchant-princes of the Renaissance, was that it should be translated into an environment of beauty and dignity, as its proper appanages; and that once the eye was trained to the pursuit, the appeal of great craftsmanship was irresistible and its ownership a justification of one's position. This point of view appears in Morgan, Widener, Hearst, Walters, and others of the omnivorous collectors of the first rank. It is suffused with the glow of American pragmatism, which was also the pragmatism of the Fuggers and the Medici."

The sales in the previous year of Impressionist and Postimpressionist pictures from the collection of Margaret Biddle, in Paris, and of Jacob Goldschmidt, in London, were the first auctions at which the art-collecting boom of the 1960s, 1970s, and 1980s began to be felt. For the first time in years, there was strong international competition for modern masterpieces and prices that would have pleased even those formidable dealers of previous generations Ernest Gambart and Joseph Duveen.

In New York, the Lurcy sale was the event that ushered in the new era in collecting and big-time auctions. Georges Lurcy (1891–1953), a wealthy financier, had left Paris just before the outbreak of World War II with his American wife and his impressive art collection. By the war's end they were ensconced in a mansion at 813 Fifth Avenue and an estate on Long Island.

After Georges Lurcy's death, a sale was planned, then postponed, and by the time it took place, an ever-growing number of collectors had begun to manifest a desire to possess artworks Lurcy had owned. The flurry of excitement that built up before the auction was enormous. Closed-circuit television was used for the first time at Parke-Bernet to accommodate an overflow audience of notables, who paid $1,708,500 for sixty-five paintings at the evening sale and $2,200,000 for the decorative arts and furnishings in the afternoon sessions. Parke-Bernet and the New York auction market were on the threshold of a new age.

One of a pair of carved, painted, and parcel-gilt wood commodes, attributed to Joachim Dietrich, after a design by François Cuvilliès. South German (probably Munich), c. 1745. Height 33″. The J. Paul Getty Museum, Malibu, California. Lot 383 in the sale of furniture and decorative arts from the collection of Georges Lurcy, at Parke-Bernet Galleries, November 8–9, 1957. Each commode sold for $14,000.

The sale catalogue attributed the design of this delightful piece to François Cuvilliès (1695–1768), the architect-decorator who was responsible for redoing in the rococo style the interiors of the Residenz in Munich, where Cuvilliès' most famous creation, the court theater, has been masterfully restored to its original glory.

Oriental pearl necklace with fifty-five matched pearls weighing together about 851 grains. Private collection. This and a companion strand were lots 114 and 116 in the Mrs. John Rovensky jewelry auction at Parke-Bernet Galleries on January 23, 1957. This lot sold for $90,000, the other for $61,000.

So splendid were these necklaces considered that they were valued at more than a million dollars in 1916, when Mrs. Rovensky (then Mrs. Morton Plant) exchanged her house at Fifth Avenue and Fifty-second Street for them. Mrs. Plant moved up to Eighty-sixth Street with her necklaces; Cartier, Inc., is still in business in the former Plant house. Real estate proved a better investment than Oriental pearls, the market for which was severely depressed by the development of the cultured-pearl industry. Also auctioned at this time was Mrs. Rovensky's fabulous diamond necklace, which brought an impressive $360,000.

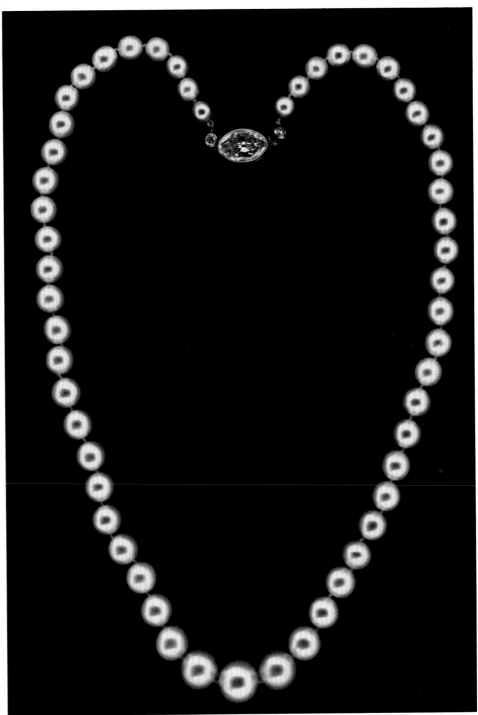

Formerly, the Morton Plant residence at Fifth Avenue and Fifty-second Street, New York; now the Cartier Building.

Henri de Toulouse-Lautrec. *Aristide Bruant aux Ambassadeurs.* c. 1892. Gouache and watercolor on paper, mounted on canvas, 54½ x 36½". Private collection. Lot 56 in the auction of Georges Lurcy's collection of Impressionist and modern paintings, held at Parke-Bernet Galleries on November 7, 1957. It sold for $62,000.

This drawing is related to Toulouse-Lautrec's famous poster of the same subject and depicts Aristide Bruant, a popular café singer of the 1880s and 1890s, who became a good friend of the artist's. Bruant's characteristic costume included black velvet jacket and wide-brimmed black hat, and, always, the red scarf.

1958

Camille Pissarro. *Landscape near Pontoise: The Auvers Road.* 1881. Oil on canvas, 21¼ x 35½". Private collection. Lot 8 in the sale of Impressionist and modern paintings from the Arnold Kirkeby collection, at Parke-Bernet Galleries, November 19, 1958. The price at that time was $62,500.

In 1980 the picture was sold again, in the auction of the André Meyer collection, at Sotheby Parke Bernet, New York. This time, the price was $528,000*.

Pissarro (1830–1903) spent much time in Pontoise from the mid-1860s on, and he painted many scenes of the area around the village.

The Kirkeby auction was among the important Impressionist sales that took place in the mid-to-late 1950s. Each one showed advances in the price levels of pictures that had supplanted completely in the affections of fashionable collectors the Old Masters and Barbizon works so much admired in decades past. The continued growth of the popularity of the Impressionists may be gauged by the auction price in 1980 of the illustrated painting.

In the Kirkeby auction of 1958, a Picasso painting fetched $152,000, at the time the highest auction price ever paid in America for the work of a living artist.

1959

Alaska and Hawaii become the forty-ninth and fiftieth states to join the Union.

Saint Lawrence Seaway opens to shipping.

The Tin Drum by Günter Grass, *Goodbye Columbus* by Philip Roth, and *The Zoo Story* by Edward Albee are published.

Just two months after Major Hiram Parke died, the firm he had shepherded through two decades of sales held one of the most successful affairs in its history. The auction of the superb collections of pictures, furniture, ceramics, and bibelots from the estate of Thelma Chrysler Foy was the high point of the year. Dealers and collectors from all over the world bid furiously for the seventeen Impressionist and modern pictures in a gala evening auction that brought in more than a million dollars. Record prices were set on May 13 for the paintings and on subsequent afternoons for many of the objects in the sessions devoted to decorative arts and books. The two hardcover catalogues describing the objects in Mrs. Foy's collection were appropriately bound in the same distinctive white-and-gold colors that had been the main theme of her apartment, which had provided such a sympathetic background for the treasures displayed there.

Louis XV inlaid mahogany writing table with marquetry, attributed to Bernard van Risenburgh. French, eighteenth century. Height 31″. Private collection, Europe. Lot 307 in a sale of French furniture and decorative arts held at Parke-Bernet on November 13–14, 1959, fetched $37,000.

In 1979 this *bureau plat* was sold for $452,300 at Sotheby Parke Bernet in Monte Carlo at the auction of the collection of Akram Ojjeh.

Furniture by Bernard van Risenburgh (c. 1700–1765/7), known to collectors only by his initials B.V.R.B. until the mid-1950s, when the identity of this master *ébéniste* was established, has always been highly desirable and expensive. This table was once owned by the famous collector Rodolphe Kann of Paris; later it entered the collections of Sir Joseph Duveen, Collis P. Huntington, and then Yale University.

Pieces from a Sèvres porcelain monogrammed dessert service. French, 1771–72. The Metropolitan Museum of Art, New York. The Wrightsman Collection.

A forty-piece dessert service was sold as lot 431 in the Thelma Chrysler Foy auction on May 16, 1959, for $60,000.

Louis René Edouard, the Cardinal-Prince de Rohan (1734–1803), commissioned the service in 1771 and brought it with him to Vienna, where he was sent as ambassador in 1772. The full service originally comprised 368 pieces and cost 20,772 livres. Later, the cardinal-prince's involvement in the notorious affair of the diamond necklace of Queen Marie Antoinette led to his downfall and banishment from court.

Pierre Auguste Renoir. *The Daughters of Durand-Ruel*. 1882. Oil on canvas, 32 x 25¾". The Chrysler Museum, Norfolk, Virginia. Gift of Walter P. Chrysler, Jr. Lot 15 in the Thelma Chrysler Foy sale of May 13, 15, and 16, 1959, fetched $255,000.

Renoir's portrait of the two daughters of his dealer, patron, and friend, Paul Durand-Ruel, was shown in New York at the historic Impressionist Exhibition held in 1886 at the American Art Association on East Twenty-third Street. It was first owned by the husband of one of Durand-Ruel's daughters and was later acquired by Mrs. Foy. After her death, at the auction of the Foy collection, it was bought by Mrs. Foy's brother, Walter P. Chrysler. A great art collector in his own right, Chrysler was later the chief benefactor of the museum in Norfolk, Virginia, that was renamed after him in recognition of his generosity.

1960

John F. Kennedy is elected thirty-fifth president of the United States.

New planned city of Brasília becomes the capital of Brazil.

Myron C. Taylor (1874–1959) was an attorney and a textile manufacturer before he succeeded J. P. Morgan as chairman of the board of directors of the U.S. Steel Corporation. In this capacity he persuaded his board to accept collective bargaining with the steelworkers' union in 1937, thus avoiding labor problems during a crucial period for American industry. From 1939 to 1950, Taylor served as President Roosevelt's personal representative to the Vatican, holding the rank of ambassador. He also served on many charitable and philanthropic boards, including that of the Metropolitan Museum of Art.

The Myron and Annabel Taylor auction was of a type that was becoming increasingly rare each year, the single-family collection with thousands of lots of fine and decorative arts of all types: Gothic, Renaissance, eighteenth century, American, English, Oriental, Old Masters, ancestor portraits, modern drawings—all collected by one individual or married couple.

As most present-day auction catalogues indicate, collections tend to be smaller and more specialized in scope as a result of changed attitudes and concerns—about taxes, insurance, security, and aesthetic purity—that seemed far less important to collectors of an earlier era.

Andrea della Robbia. *Saint Michael the Archangel*. c. 1475. Glazed terra-cotta, height 31⅛″. The Metropolitan Museum of Art, New York. Harris Brisbane Dick Fund, 1960. Lot 899 in the Myron and Annabel Taylor collection sale at Parke-Bernet, November 11–12, 1960. It brought $40,000.

The lunette had originally been installed over the main door of the church of St. Michael in Faenza.

172

Late Gothic millefleurs armorial tapestry. Tournai(?), 1487–1501. 12′ x 12′1″. The Metropolitan Museum of Art. The Cloisters Collection, Purchase, 1960. Lot 1019 in the Myron and Annabel Taylor sale, November 11–12, 1960, was bought by the Metropolitan Museum for $32,500.

The arms included in the design of this tapestry indicate it was made for Lord Dynham, who became a Knight of the Garter in 1487.

Like the Unicorn Tapestries, also in the Metropolitan Museum, this textile is of a type called "millefleurs," after the multitude of vigorously flowering plants that fill the background. No fewer than ten important Gothic tapestries hung in the Taylor house at 16 East Seventieth Street. Like so many of New York's private residences, it was demolished and replaced by an apartment house.

1961

Although the high prices achieved by Impressionist paintings at auctions during the late 1950s had an impact on the relatively few collectors who were interested in the subject, it was the worldwide publicity generated by the unprecedented prices achieved at the Alfred Erickson sale that helped to bring about a popular boom in art appreciation and collecting during the 1960s. An increasingly affluent and better-educated public was predisposed to be impressed by the magical combination of an enormous price, the most that had ever been fetched by a painting at auction, paid by a prominent cultural institution for a stunningly dramatic painting of historic interest, *Aristotle Contemplating the Bust of Homer,* by one of Europe's most famous artists.

Within a day or two of the auction, stories about the sale appeared in newspapers everywhere. Immediately, lines began to form at the Metropolitan Museum as thousands waited to see the painting that was the focus of all the attention. The picture—its glamor, beauty, and price—captured the public imagination as had no other work of art since 1889, when Millet's *Angelus* arrived at the American Art Association.

Of course, there were those who condemned the vulgarity of linking the sacred (art) and the profane (money), and there were others who professed unease and revulsion at the high price. But, for better or worse, a shot had been fired that was heard round the world: art collecting, art museums, and art auctions would never be the same again.

Left: Jean-Honoré Fragonard. *A Young Girl Reading.* c. 1776. Oil on canvas, 32 x 25½". National Gallery of Art, Washington, D.C. Gift of Mrs. Mellon Bruce in memory of her father, Andrew W. Mellon, 1961. Lot 16 in the Alfred W. Erickson sale, November 15, 1961. Its price was $875,000.

Jean-Honoré Fragonard (1737–1806) is the acknowledged master of the intimate eighteenth-century portrait-study, of which there are so many fine examples. *A Young Girl Reading* is among the most popular pictures on view at the National Gallery.

Opposite: Rembrandt Harmensz. van Rijn. *Aristotle Contemplating the Bust of Homer.* 1653. Oil on canvas, 56½ x 53¾". The Metropolitan Museum of Art, New York. Purchased with special funds and gifts of friends of the Museum, 1961. Lot 7 in the landmark auction of the Alfred W. Erickson collection at Parke-Bernet Galleries, November 15, 1961. It was bought for $2.3 million.

Alfred W. Erickson (d. 1936), co-founder of the McCann-Erickson Advertising Agency, acquired Rembrandt's *Aristotle* from Duveen Brothers in 1929. After the Wall Street Crash, he sold the picture back to Duveen; a year or so later he reacquired the painting, at a net cost to himself of more than $1 million. *Aristotle* and twenty-three other Old Master pictures hung in the Erickson house on Murray Hill in New York City until Mrs. Erickson's death in 1961. Their entire collection brought $4,679,250.

Chippendale cherrywood blockfront chest of drawers carved with a shell motif. American, New London County, Connecticut, 1770–90. Height 36¾″. The Edison Institute, Henry Ford Museum and Greenfield Village, Dearborn, Michigan. Lot 130 in the sale of American furniture and decorative arts from the Reginald Lewis collection, Parke-Bernet Galleries, March 24–25, 1961. The chest sold for $13,000.

The eighteenth-century blockfront case pieces with carved shell ornaments that are so rare and expensive today were for the most part made in Newport, Rhode Island, but the tradition existed in Connecticut as well, with interesting regional variations and eccentricities.

In the Reginald Lewis sale of Americana, prices could be compared favorably with those achieved during the 1920s and early 1930s. Since 1961 the market has continued to rise steadily.

Chinese export porcelain blue-and-white plate decorated with the Order of the Cincinnati, from the George Washington service. c. 1785. Diameter 9½″. Private collection.

A similar plate was included in the Reginald Lewis American furniture and decorative arts sale held at Parke-Bernet on March 24–25, 1961, when it brought $5,000. In 1974 another plate from the service brought $12,000 in New York at a Sotheby Parke Bernet sale.

Washington's extensive dinner service, made to order in China, was decorated with the emblem of the Order of the Cincinnati, a society formed in 1783 whose membership was restricted to officers of the Continental armies who had served under Washington and were now returning to their homes to become civilians at the close of the Revolutionary War. The order was named after the Roman general Lucius Quinctius Cincinnatus, who resumed life as a farmer after his military duties were completed.

Above: Alessandro Vittoria. Set of four gilded bronze statuettes of the Evangelists. Height 11½". Private collection. Lot 189 in the auction on June 27–28, 1962, of the collection of Miss Julia A. Berwind at her home, "The Elms," in Newport, Rhode Island *(left)*—one of the greatest house sales ever managed by Parke-Bernet.

"The Elms" had been built in 1901 for Miss Berwind's brother, Edward J. Berwind, and was filled with costly furnishings. Tapestries and marble statues adorned the grand staircase, and the size and magnificence of this palatial Newport "cottage" were overwhelming.

In addition to the indispensable oversized Chinese vases, gilt furniture, and marble embellishments, there was a small but fine group of Renaissance works of art, including this exceptional set of statuettes by Alessandro Vittoria (1525–1608), a leading monumental sculptor in Venice. The set brought $8,000.

"The Elms" is now open to the public under the auspices of the Preservation Society of Newport County.

1963

President John F. Kennedy is assassinated in Dallas.

Beatles achieve worldwide popularity.

Gold and enamel peach-form watch, by William Ilbery. London, c. 1820. Length 3⅜″. The Time Museum, Rockford, Illinois. Lot 91 in the sale of watches from the collection of Charles H. Morse of Lake Forest, Illinois, at Parke-Bernet Galleries on February 8, 1963. It brought $1,600—which would be a ridiculously low figure today. The demand for watches, which has since grown tremendously here and abroad, had a very long way to go in 1963.

Intricate and elaborate watches have been made, and have been prized by collectors, since the days of the Renaissance. This peach-form watch, though made in England, was probably intended for the export market.

Frans Hals. *The Merry Lute Player.* c. 1625–27. Oil on cradled panel, 35½ x 29½″. Private collection, London. Lot 10 in the auction of Old Masters from the collection of Oscar B. Cintas on May 1, 1963, at Parke-Bernet Galleries. It was bought by E. Speelman of London for $600,000.

In 1944 *The Merry Lute Player* had been acquired by Cintas at Parke-Bernet for $127,000. Cintas (1887–1957), who in years past had purchased Lincoln memorabilia at Parke-Bernet, served as Cuban ambassador to the United States.

Frans Hals (1585–1666) was famous during his lifetime but forgotten until the late nineteenth century, when his brilliance was rediscovered by artists and collectors. His popularity has continued to grow.

Willem de Kooning. *Two Standing Women*. 1949. Oil on canvas, 29½ x 26¼″. The Irwin and Bethea Green collection. Lot 54 in the Larry Aldrich collection sale of October 25, 1963, at Parke-Bernet Galleries (purchased by Norton Simon for $27,000). This was the first major work by de Kooning (b. 1904) to appear at auction. In 1970, the Norton Simon Foundation sold *Two Standing Women* at Sotheby Parke Bernet, New York, for $45,000.

Larry Aldrich, a noted collector of modern paintings and sculptures, is the founder of a museum of contemporary art in Ridgefield, Connecticut.

David Smith. *Raven IV.* 1957. Steel, height 28⅛″. Hirshhorn Museum and Sculpture Garden, Smithsonian Institution, Washington, D.C. Lot 50 in a sale of modern art on November 18, 1964, at Parke-Bernet Galleries, which had become affiliated in July with Sotheby & Co., London. The price: $4,750.

This was the second time a work by the American artist David Smith (1906–1965) had appeared at a New York auction. His sculptures did not begin to achieve high prices until after his death.

Smith wrote in 1953: "Very often, I seem to be much more concerned with the monsters than with what are called beauties.... I don't feel at all like the age of Graces.... I don't think this is an age of Grace." His sculptures have been recognized as masterful expressions of the age, and he is generally considered among the great artists of his generation.

1965

Joan Miró. *Circus Horse*. 1927. Oil and pencil on burlap, 76¾ x 100⅜". Hirshhorn Museum and Sculpture Garden, Smithsonian Institution, Washington, D.C. Lot 18 in the sale of important contemporary art belonging to Philippe Dotrement of Brussels held on April 14, 1965, at Sotheby Parke Bernet, New York. The work realized $57,500.

The Dotrement collection contained both European and American abstract works and was the first Continental collection of twentieth-century contemporary art sold at auction in New York. Miró (1893–1983), a Catalan painter and sculptor, was an important figure in the Surrealist movement.

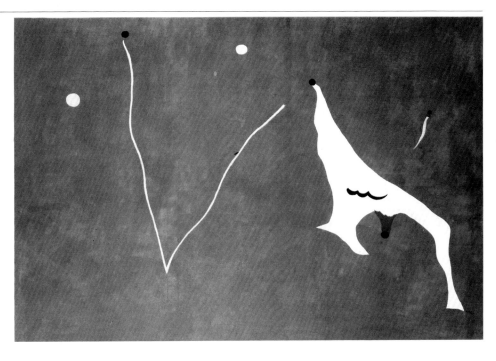

Edouard Vuillard. *Portrait of the Comtesse de Noailles*. c. 1930–32. Oil on canvas, 43½ x 50½". Mr. and Mrs. Samuel J. LeFrak collection, New York. Lot 70 in the sale of Impressionist and modern art held on April 14, 1965, at Sotheby Parke Bernet, New York, brought $74,000.

Anne Elisabeth Mathieu de Noailles (1876–1933) was celebrated for her beauty, her charm, and her literary accomplishments. She wrote lyrical poetry, and her autobiography, *Le livre de ma vie,* was published in 1932.

Guests at the gala dinner held on the evening of April 14, 1965, in the exhibition galleries at 980 Madison Avenue during the intermission between the Impressionist sale and the Dotrement sale. The dinner's theme was a Parisian café, and the proceeds benefited the English-Speaking Union—an apt confluence of nationalities at a sale held in America, at a by-now British-owned auction gallery, and devoted in the main to French works of art.

The evening of April 14, one of the most exciting and unusual in the history of the firm, put the Sotheby stamp on the Parke-Bernet tradition of gala evening sales, to the delight of a responsive and increasingly international audience of collectors and dealers.

Wrought-gold and enamel "serpent and egg" rotary clock set with diamonds (Duchess of Marlborough Clock), designed by Peter Karl Fabergé, executed under the direction of workmaster Mikhail Perchin. St. Petersburg, 1902. Height 9¼". The Forbes Magazine Collection, New York. Lot 326 in the auction of French furniture and decorative arts belonging to Madame Ganna Walska, at Sotheby Parke Bernet, New York, on May 14–15, 1965. The clock was sold for $50,000.

Walska had been an opera singer and was living in retirement in Santa Barbara, California, at the date of the sale. The price for her important clock set a record for Fabergé. In 1902 the Duchess of Marlborough (née Consuelo Vanderbilt) commissioned this timepiece from Fabergé while she and her husband were on a tour of Russia. It was sold by Madame Jacques Balsan (formerly the Duchess of Marlborough) in 1926 at a benefit auction in Paris to aid the hospital at Vincennes.

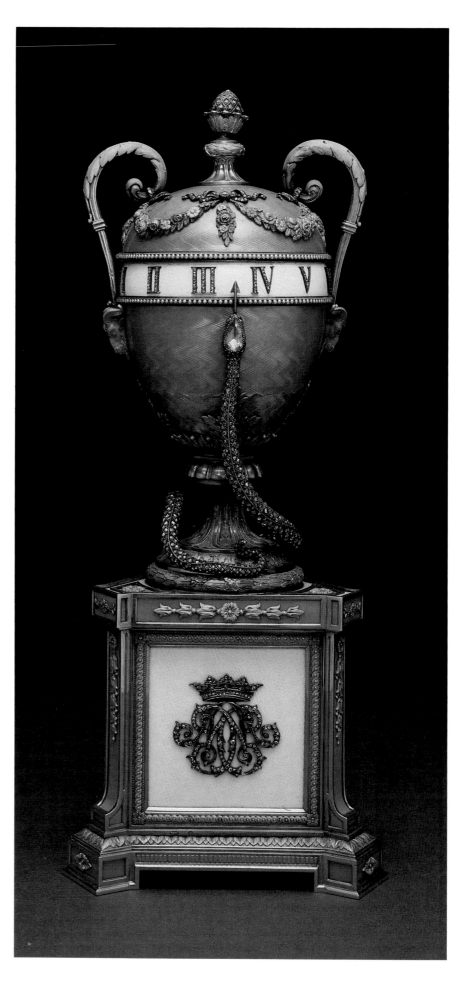

1966

Cultural Revolution begins in China as Chairman Mao purges dissidents with the help of Red Guards.

Founder of a worldwide cosmetic empire, Helena Rubinstein ("Madame" to her family, friends, and employees) was truly a legend in her own time. Thus, it is not surprising that the dispersal of her various collections at Sotheby Parke Bernet, New York, in the spring of 1966 attracted considerable attention. Hers was the most personal and unusual group of sales held in New York in many years. Paintings, works of art, and furnishings from Rubinstein's homes in Paris, London, and New York were gathered together in the galleries at 980 Madison Avenue for a week of auctions described in five separate catalogues.

African art and African-period Picassos, Egyptian antiquities, Victorian settees, Russian icons, and Matisse etchings were among the incredible assortment of objects on view. The auctions gave the opportunity to a new generation of collectors to explore the interests and tastes of a dynamic and adventurous woman who seems always to have been in the right place at the right time, both in her brilliant business career and in her art-collecting activities.

Imperial Russian nuptial crown set with diamonds. c. 1800. Height 5¾". Hillwood, Washington, D.C. Lot 155 in a sale on December 6–7, 1966, at Sotheby Parke Bernet, New York, of antique and modern precious-stone jewelry from the estate of Helen M. de Kay, New York. The crown, containing 1,535 "old-mine" diamonds, sold for $77,500. According to tradition, it was worn at their weddings by Russian empresses from Maria Alexandrovna (1824–1880) to Alexandra Feodorovna (1872–1918), who is depicted wearing the tiara in 1894 in a painting by Laurits Tuxen now in Buckingham Palace. The stones are believed to have been taken from a diamond-studded belt of Catherine the Great.

Graham Sutherland. *Helena Rubinstein in Red Brocade Balenciaga Gown*. 1957. Oil on canvas, 61 x 36". Helena Rubinstein Foundation, New York.

Carved wood dance mask. Northern Dan, Yakaba region, Ivory Coast. Height 10¼". Private collection. Lot 9 in the sale of African art from the estate of Helena Rubinstein held at Sotheby Parke Bernet, New York, on April 21, 1966. It sold for $1,650.

In 1977 this piece was part of the Mr. and Mrs. Morris J. Pinto collection, sold at Sotheby's, London. The mask then fetched $28,050. The Rubinstein auction was the first major sale of African art held in New York.

Elie Nadelman. *Classical Head.* c. 1909–11. White marble, height 12⅜". Hirshhorn Museum and Sculpture Garden, Smithsonian Institution, Washington, D.C. Lot 18 in the Helena Rubinstein sale at Sotheby Parke Bernet, New York, on April 20, 1966, fetched $4,250.

Helena Rubinstein's patronage was crucial to Nadelman's early success. Like his patroness, Nadelman (1882–1946) was born in Poland, and his first one-man show, at Patterson's Gallery in London in 1911, was purchased in toto by Rubinstein. After settling in the United States, Nadelman became fascinated with American folk art, and his later work is far less classical in feeling than the early marble pieces.

Tiffany red favrile-glass cabinet vase. c. 1912. Height 3¾". Private collection. Lot 53 in the auction of Tiffany glass from the Coats-Connelly collection, held at Sotheby Parke Bernet, New York, on October 21, 1966. It sold for $900.

In 1982, when the vase was in the collection of Barbara and Philip Hoover, it again was sold at Sotheby Parke Bernet, this time for $3,300.

The auction of favrile and other glass made in the studios of Louis Comfort Tiffany, from the collection of James Coats and Brian Connelly, was the first to indicate that Tiffany's reputation (and the prices his works could command) had begun to rise dramatically. Subsequently, the improved market drew so many fine Tiffany lamps and other objects to the auction rooms that new records seemed to be reached every few months.

The year's auctions included one of the first successful sales of photographs and the dispersal of the Thomas Streeter library of Americana, at which the *Cambridge Platform* of 1649, a defense of New England's church-dominated government, brought $80,000.

An increasingly heated market for Impressionist and modern paintings and sculpture was also much in evidence. The art boom of the 1960s and 1970s was now in full swing and Sotheby Parke Bernet was very much in the thick of it.

Gold and black enamel "High Society" cigarette case set with diamonds. c. 1956. Private collection. Lot 40 in the sale on May 17, 1967, at Sotheby Parke Bernet, New York, of Cole Porter's collection of presentation cases and boxes, which he had left to the New York Public Library's Theater Collection at Lincoln Center. This box brought $4,000.

Cole Porter (1893–1964) received from his wife, Linda, a specially designed case upon the occasion of the opening of each of his musical plays, including *Gay Divorce, Born to Dance, Dubarry Was a Lady,* and *Kiss Me Kate,* from 1930 to 1953. In 1956, upon the completion of the film *High Society,* Porter had this box made for himself, Mrs. Porter having died in 1954.

The auction was a nostalgic event and it drew a large crowd of theater people and benefactors of the Library's Theater Collection.

Caricature sketch of Cole Porter by Al Hirschfeld, reproduced on the cover of the catalogue prepared for the auction of Mr. Porter's collection of boxes and cases on May 17, 1967.

Opposite: Jean Baptiste Camille Corot. *Young Woman in a Red Bodice Holding a Mandolin.* c. 1868–70. Oil on cradled panel, 18¼ x 14½". The Norton Simon Foundation, Pasadena, California. Lot 18 in the sale of Impressionist and modern paintings held at Sotheby Parke Bernet, New York, on October 26, 1967. The price, $310,000, was a record for Corot at the time.

This portrait, from the collection of Carl Weeks of Des Moines, Iowa, was first sold at the auction held after Corot's death, in 1875, when the contents of his atelier were dispersed at the Hôtel Drouot in Paris. In recent years, figure subjects by Corot have fetched very high prices, indicating that collectors' taste has veered away from his atmospheric landscapes so popular earlier in the century.

187

1968

Widespread rioting follows assassination of Martin Luther King, Jr., in Memphis, Tennessee.

Richard Nixon is elected president of the United States.

Environmental sculptor Christo wraps the Berne Kunsthalle.

Miss Taylor wearing her new diamond ring.

Diamond ring. Elizabeth Taylor collection. Lot 159 in a sale of precious-stone jewelry held at Sotheby Parke Bernet, New York, on May 16, 1968, when it sold for $365,000. The diamond weighs 33.19 carats. This lot received a huge amount of publicity because of the price it fetched and the buyer's celebrity.

Rembrandt Harmensz. van Rijn. *Three Gabled Cottages beside a Road.* 1650. Etching and drypoint, third state of three, 6¼ x 8″. Lot 87 in the section of the Gordon Nowell-Usticke auction of Rembrandt landscape and portrait etchings held in 1968 at Sotheby Parke Bernet, New York. The selling price was $8,000.

The collection formed by Captain Gordon Nowell-Usticke between 1934 and 1954 was one of the most important private collections of Rembrandt's graphic work ever to appear on the auction market.

Altogether comprising some 410 lots, these auctions—held in 1967 and 1968 at Sotheby Parke Bernet—had a tremendous effect on the market for Rembrandt prints. Prices were generally much higher than had been anticipated, so much so that when Nowell-Usticke's book on Rembrandt's etched work—a comprehensive survey with a history of prices—was published soon after the auction, the author appended an unbound essay entitled "An Amazing Happening," wherein he described the remarkable results of the sale and admitted that the valuations in the book were no longer applicable.

Pierre Auguste Renoir. *The Pont des Arts, Paris.*
c. 1868. Oil on canvas, 24½ x 40½". © The
Norton Simon Foundation. Norton Simon
Museum, Pasadena, California. Lot 8 in the sale
of Impressionist paintings held in New York on
October 9, 1968, at Sotheby Parke Bernet.
Consigned by Mrs. Clifford Klenk, this early
masterpiece by Renoir commanded $1.55 mil-
lion, a world-record price for any Impressionist
picture.

1969

Georges Pompidou becomes president of France after Charles de Gaulle resigns.

Neil Armstrong becomes the first man to stand on the moon.

Huge antiwar demonstrations in the United States and overseas are held to protest the Vietnam War.

One of a pair of Meissen porcelain figures of parrots, by Johann Joachim Kändler, mounted in Louis XV ormolu. c. 1745. Height 15″. Private collection. Part of lot 47 in the auction of French furniture and decorative arts from the collection of Madame Lucienne Fribourg held at Sotheby Parke Bernet, New York, on April 19, 1969.

The candelabra, which sold for $65,000 the pair, were eagerly sought after by important collectors because the figures of parrots had been modeled in 1741 by Johann Joachim Kändler (1706–1775), the acknowledged master of the Meissen factory's sculptors; moreover, the superb rococo mounts were stamped with a "crowned C," signifying a tax paid on gilt-bronze during the reign of Louis XV. This same pair had previously brought $2,600 at the Mrs. Henry Walters auction in 1941 at Parke-Bernet.

Diamond ring and necklace, designed by Harry Winston, Inc. Elizabeth Taylor collection. Lot 133 in the jewelry auction on October 23, 1969, at Sotheby Parke Bernet, New York. The ring sold for $1.05 million and the necklace—from which it may be hung as a pendant—brought $25,000.

The bidding for the ring, weighing 69.4 carats, between representatives of Cartier, Inc., and the actor Richard Burton's agent, was one of the most electrifying in auction history. The audience spontaneously rose to watch the bids fly back and forth and climb to a world-record price for a diamond—indeed, for any piece of jewelry.

The winning bid was Cartier's, but following the sale the ring and the necklace were acquired for Elizabeth Taylor Burton from the jeweler's establishment amid unprecedented publicity.

The Peregrina Pearl. Elizabeth Taylor collection. Lot 129 in a jewelry auction held on January 23, 1969. The price was $37,000 for this pear-shaped pearl, weighing about 203 grains and traditionally believed to have been in the collection of the Spanish royal family.

Louis XVI carved and painted beechwood open armchair with caning, by Georges Jacob. French, 1787. The J. Paul Getty Museum, Malibu, California. Lot 1037 in the auction held by Sotheby Parke Bernet at Newport, Rhode Island, on September 16–18, 1969, consisting of the contents of "Château-sur-Mer," the home of the Misses Edith and Maude Wetmore. It fetched $4,500.

Recent research has shown this to be a *fauteuil de toilette,* part of the suite of furniture *"de forme nouvelle . . . avec des feuilles d'acanthe"* ordered by Queen Marie Antoinette for her new "small" apartment at Versailles in 1783. The cabinetmaker, Georges Jacob (1739–1814), was one of the leading chairmakers in Paris before and after the Revolution. This armchair was carved by the firm of Triquet & Rode.

William Michael Harnett. *Mr. Hulings' Rack Picture*. 1888. Oil on canvas, 30 x 25″. Mr. and Mrs. Jacob M. Kaplan collection, New York. Lot 62 in the American painting sale held on March 19–20, 1969, at Sotheby Parke Bernet, New York, fetched $75,000.

William Michael Harnett (1848–1892), the Irish-born Philadelphia artist, was known to have done one of his two celebrated *trompe l'oeil* "rack pictures" for a friend and patron, the dry-goods merchant George Hulings, but until this canvas was consigned to Sotheby Parke Bernet in 1969, the painting had been considered lost. A work in the Museum of Modern Art, New York, by John Peto, Harnett's contemporary, also a master of the *trompe l'oeil* technique, was formerly thought to be this very painting.

Discoveries of "lost" paintings, although rare enough to be newsworthy, occur surprisingly often at auction galleries, to the delight of their owners and the pleasure of the expert who has helped to bring the vanished picture to light.

1970

Anwar al-Sadat becomes president of Egypt.

United States troops are sent to Cambodia.

Antoine Watteau. *Couple Seated on a Bank.* Red, black, and white chalk on buff paper, 9½ x 13¾″. The Armand Hammer Foundation Collection, Los Angeles. Lot 20 in the sale of Old Master drawings from the collection of Irma N. Straus, held at Sotheby Parke Bernet, New York, on October 21, 1970. The price was $65,000.

This superb example of the art of Watteau (1684–1721) was one of the most important drawings ever to be auctioned in New York. Dr. Armand Hammer acquired a number of drawings at this sale for his collection.

Page from a manuscript of the Haggadah, illuminated on vellum by Joseph Leipnik. Altona, c. 1736. Private collection. Lot 151 in the auction of the late Michael Zagayski's collection of Hebrew manuscripts and books held at Sotheby Parke Bernet, New York, on January 27–28, 1970. The price at the sale was $13,500.

On June 23, 1983, this magnificent Haggadah appeared again at a Sotheby Parke Bernet, New York, auction, when it brought a record price for a Haggadah of $290,400*.

Joseph ben David Leipnik was the most important member of the eighteenth-century school of illuminators active in Hamburg, Germany.

Judaica sales, often single-owner collections, have been a regular feature of the New York auction rooms for decades. Michael Zagayski's was one of the finest ever sold at the New York auction house.

Vincent van Gogh. *Cypress and Blossoming Tree*. 1889. Oil on canvas, 20¼ x 25½". Private collection. Lot 10 in the auction of paintings from the estate of W. W. Crocker, held at Sotheby Parke Bernet, New York, on February 25, 1970.

The picture, which set a new sale record for a work by the artist at $1.3 million, was painted by van Gogh during his confinement in the hospital at Saint-Rémy the year before his death. Late works by van Gogh are the most sought after of all his paintings, for they embody all the passion and pathos of the artist's struggles, accomplishments, and tragic death.

1971

Nineteen seventy-one could well be called the Norton Simon year at Sotheby Parke Bernet. Three of the year's most significant auctions involved this noted collector as either buyer or seller.

In the spring, an impressive group of paintings and drawings ranging from Old Masters to contemporary art from Simon's private collection and including, in addition, Chinese art, furniture, Renaissance works of art, and tapestries from the Norton Simon Foundation were sold at Sotheby Parke Bernet. For the most part, the Foundation's works consisted of the former stock of Duveen Brothers of New York, the famous Sir Joseph Duveen's firm, the remaining inventory of which had been purchased en bloc by Simon. The first Baron Duveen of Millbank (Sir Joseph's title) had been one of the key figures in the history of collecting during the first half of the twentieth century. He died in 1939, but the New York branch of his firm continued in business for some twenty years longer.

Henri Rousseau. *Exotic Landscape*. 1910. Oil on canvas, 51¼ x 64″. The Norton Simon Foundation, Pasadena, California. Lot 90 in the auction of Impressionist and modern art held at Sotheby Parke Bernet, New York, on October 21, 1971, bought by Simon for $775,000.

From the collection of Mrs. Robert McCormick of Chicago and Washington, D.C., *Exotic Landscape* was one of the most important works by Henri ("Douanier") Rousseau ever to have appeared at auction.

The Lord of the Manor, late Gothic tapestry. Tournai, 1475–1500. 11′4″ x 13′. Lot 224 in the sale of works of art from the Norton Simon Foundation, May 7–8, 1971, at Sotheby Parke Bernet, New York. The price was $45,000.

Although the firm of Duveen Brothers specialized in Old Master paintings and English eighteenth-century portraits (for example, *The Blue Boy* by Gainsborough, now in the Huntington Library and Art Gallery in San Marino, California), its holdings of French furniture and sculpture, Renaissance works of art, and fine tapestries were impressive indeed.

Many European works of art that had found their way to America would be "repatriated" by dealers and collectors bidding at New York auctions as the European economies continued to prosper and as the fashion for these objects, which had flowed into America during the 1920s in quantity, continued to wane in America except among institutional buyers.

Hilaire Germain Edgar Degas. *Little Dancer, Age Fourteen.* 1880. Bronze, muslin, and satin ribbon, height 37½″. Belle Linsky collection, New York. Lot 29 in the sale of nineteenth- and twentieth-century art from the private collection of Norton Simon, held at Sotheby Parke Bernet, New York, on May 5, 1971. The price was $380,000.

Degas undertook his *Petite Danseuse* for the Impressionist group show of 1880 but did not complete it in time for that exhibition. When finally shown in 1881, it caused considerable controversy because Degas used real satin and muslin for the costume. The model was a student from the children's ballet class at the Paris Opera.

1972

Richard Nixon, reelected president, visits the People's Republic of China.

Feminist movement gains strength in the United States.

Over the years Cranbrook Academy of Art, in Bloomfield Hills, Michigan, an important center for education in the fine and applied arts, including architecture and furniture and textile design, acquired a wide-ranging collection of art objects. In 1972 the trustees decided to sell a number of these at Sotheby Parke Bernet in order to raise funds to carry out the institution's fundamental teaching role, a role that has recently received wide recognition through the international traveling exhibition *Design in America: The Cranbrook Vision, 1925–1950,* sponsored by the Metropolitan Museum of Art, New York, and the Detroit Institute of Arts.

Henry Moore. *Reclining Figure.* c. 1945–46. Carved elmwood, length 75″. Private collection. Lot 21 in a sale of modern sculpture on March 1, 1972, at Sotheby Parke Bernet, New York. *Reclining Figure* brought $260,000, at that time a world-record price for a sculpture by a living artist.

Exactly ten years later, in May 1982, *Reclining Figure* was auctioned again at Sotheby Parke Bernet for $1,265,000*, yet another world-record price for a sculpture by a living artist—but also the highest sum ever paid for any modern sculpture.

Henry Moore (b. 1898) mentions in his writings that this sculpture had, for him "great drama, with its big beating heart like a pumping station."

Grave Stele with Three Figures. Greek (Attica), c. 360–350 B.C. Marble, height 38¾". Norton Simon Collection.

On May 2–5, 1972, Cranbrook Academy, Michigan, offered for sale at Sotheby Parke Bernet a number of examples of Art Nouveau and Art Deco, American paintings, Oriental art, and antiquities. Norton Simon bought this stele (lot 326) for $155,000.

Relief-molded and painted black-ground porcelain dragon vase. Chinese, reign of Yong-
zheng, c. 1730. Height 12½″. Private collection.
Lot 330 in the auction of Chinese art at Sotheby
Parke Bernet, New York, on December 5,
1972. The price was $2,900.

In 1956, at the Allen J. Mercher sale at Parke-
Bernet, this vase brought $525; and in 1978, at
an auction held at Sotheby Parke Bernet in
Hong Kong, it fetched $19,000.

1973

Watergate Hearings are televised in the United States; Vice President Spiro Agnew resigns.

Britain, Ireland, and Denmark join the Common Market.

Pablo Picasso dies in France.

In March and October, paintings and sculptures owned by two astute collectors of modern American art were put on the block. Edith Gregor Halpert, owner and director of the Downtown Gallery in New York, had been one of the most important American art dealers during the middle decades of the twentieth century. Not only did she continue to handle the sales of many artists in Alfred Stieglitz's stable (for example, John Marin, Marsden Hartley, Charles Demuth, and Max Weber), but she also helped to stimulate interest in the collecting and appreciation of American folk art. The dispersal of her collection following her death was a momentous occasion for American collectors, comparable in scope, quality, and resonance to the Thomas B. Clarke sale of 1899.

At the Halpert auction Japanese bidders paid enormous prices for the paintings of Yasuo Kuniyoshi, a Japanese-American artist whose work was handled by Mrs. Halpert's gallery. High prices were also achieved at the landmark auction of important works by leading figures in contemporary American art that had been purchased by Robert Scull, a New York taxi-fleet owner, for much lower prices before the painters had earned major reputations. Several of these artists protested loudly at the sale about the alleged unfairness of the situation, in sharp contrast to Winslow Homer in 1899, when his *Eight Bells* sold for a large sum at the Thomas B. Clarke sale, enhancing the painter's reputation. Additionally, there were protests from feminists and taxi drivers, and all of the excitement gave the Scull auction the atmosphere of a major "happening" reminiscent of the 1960s, the decade in which a great many of the works in the sale had been created.

Japanese steel sword *(koto-tachi)*, by Aoe Suke-tsugu (detail). Signed and dated in the sixth month of *Showa* (1312). Private collection. Lot 396 in an auction of Japanese swords, fittings, and armor held at Sotheby Parke Bernet, New York, on May 31, 1973. The price, an astounding $70,000, reflected the rarity of this early blade, which was illustrated in a book of Japanese national treasures produced in 1935 *(Nippon to-koza).* In 1973 the sword was consigned at Sotheby's by a former military officer who had acquired it after the war in Japan.

Louise Moillon. *A Still Life of Fruit.* Oil on panel, 28 x 41″. Private collection. Lot 38 in an Old Master painting sale on December 6, 1973, at Sotheby Parke Bernet, New York. The price was much more than had been expected, at $120,000.

Louise Moillon (1610–1696) was one of the most accomplished still-life painters of early seventeenth-century France, even though, as a woman and a Huguenot, she encountered obstacles in gaining recognition.

Jasper Johns. *Painted Bronze*. 1960. Height 7½".
Ludwig Collection, Aachen, on loan to the
Kunstmuseum, Basel. Lot 16 in the famous
auction of contemporary art from the Robert
Scull collection, held on October 18, 1973, at
Sotheby Parke Bernet, New York, brought
$90,000.

These ale cans were made in an edition of two
casts—this one, and another which is in the
artist's possession.

Charles Demuth. *Love, Love, Love (Homage to Gertrude Stein).* c. 1928. Oil on board, 19½ x 23½". Thyssen-Bornemisza Collection, Lugano. Lot 47 in the Edith Gregor Halpert collection of American art, auctioned by Sotheby Parke Bernet, New York, on March 14–15, 1973. The price: $32,500.

Charles Demuth (1883–1935), more often thought of in connection with watercolor still lifes and Precisionist cityscapes, painted a number of "poster portraits," as he called them, of his friends, including Georgia O'Keeffe, Eugene O'Neill, William Carlos Williams, and, in this illustration, Gertrude Stein, the famous American expatriate writer and collector, whom Demuth had first met in Paris in 1910. The American Pop artist Robert Indiana was inspired by Demuth's Stein and Williams poster portraits to paint, among the other works for which he has become so famous, *Love.*

1974

Pair of Chippendale carved mahogany side chairs, attributed to Thomas Affleck. Philadelphia, c. 1770. Private collection.

These were two of a set of five "hairy paw-foot" side chairs found in England and sent for sale at Sotheby Parke Bernet in New York, November 12–16, 1974. A pair brought $90,000; a single chair fetched $47,500. Another, the sixth from the same set, brought $275,000* at a Sotheby's, New York, auction on October 23, 1982.

John Cadwalader, the first owner of the chairs, was one of the richest and most discerning of the eighteenth-century Philadelphia merchant-princes. He patronized several of that city's most accomplished cabinet- and chairmakers, among them William Savery, Benjamin Randolph, and Thomas Affleck (1740–1795). Once thought to be by Benjamin Randolph, these splendidly elegant and robust chairs have recently been attributed to Thomas Affleck alone.

1975

Jean-Antoine Houdon. *Portrait Bust of Benjamin Franklin*. 1779. Marble, height 16½". British Rail Pension Fund Collection, England. Lot 124 in an auction of works of art from the collection of the late Geraldine Rockefeller Dodge on November 29, 1975, at Sotheby Parke Bernet, New York. The sculpture brought $310,000.

Houdon, the sculptor-portraitist of so many prominent figures of the eighteenth century (among them, Voltaire, Washington, Jefferson, and Mirabeau), did two busts of Franklin. One, dated 1778, is in the Metropolitan Museum of Art; the other, from the Erskine Hewitt collection and later the Dodge collection, is dated 1779. Both were done from life while Franklin was America's diplomatic representative in Paris.

Auction of the collections of Geraldine Rockefeller Dodge at "Giralda," the Dodge estate in Madison, New Jersey, on October 7–11, 1975.

The dispersal—at "Giralda," near Madison, New Jersey, and then at a series of specialized auctions at Sotheby Parke Bernet during the fall of 1975 and spring of 1976—of the estate of Geraldine Rockefeller Dodge was among the largest and most important single-owner auctions in the firm's history in terms of attendance, number of pieces sold, and total amount realized (more than $9 million).

Mrs. Dodge (1872–1973) was the daughter of William Rockefeller, president of the Standard Oil Company (and brother of John D. Rockefeller), who left some $200 million to his four children when he died in 1923. When Mrs. Dodge married Marcellus Hartley Dodge in 1907, they were referred to by journalists as "the richest young couple in the world." Mrs. Dodge had two major interests: art collecting and dog breeding; and very often her works of art reflected her love of animals: for example, her beloved Barye bronzes and her paintings by Rosa Bonheur and Sir Edwin Landseer.

Mrs. Dodge's wealth, interests, background, many charitable gifts to the Madison community, and vast estate made her a celebrity during her long life, and the sale of her house and its contents drew large crowds of friends, admirers, acquaintances, and the idly curious. With the sale, an epoch in American social history seemed to have come to an end.

Ruby and diamond necklace. Private collection. Lot 273 in the auction of jewelry from the collection of Geraldine Rockefeller Dodge at Sotheby Parke Bernet, New York, on October 15, 1975. The necklace brought $330,000.

Sir Edwin Henry Landseer. *Alpine Mastiffs Reanimating a Distressed Traveler.* 1820. Oil on canvas, 74 x 93″. The Warner Collection of Gulf States Paper Corporation, Tuscaloosa, Alabama. Lot 54 in the auction of Mrs. Dodge's nineteenth-century European paintings, Sotheby Parke Bernet, New York, December 5, 1975. The price was $22,000.

This youthful work by Landseer (1802–1873) was the artist's largest and most ambitious effort to that time. The dogs are St. Bernards, from the famous monastery-hospice of the same name in the Swiss Alps.

Landseer was extremely famous and successful during his lifetime, but—along with such French animal painters as Rosa Bonheur—his works were later ridiculed and almost totally neglected until very recently. Mrs. Dodge owned eighteen Landseers and fifty Bonheurs. Price levels for these pictures were surprisingly and consistently high.

United States Bicentennial is celebrated; numerous exhibitions spur new interest in American art and antiques.

James Earl (Jimmy) Carter is elected president of the United States.

Alexander Calder, famous for his mobile sculpture, dies.

Paul Revere (1735–1818), called "the Patriot" to distinguish him from his father, who was also a silversmith, was immortalized for generations of schoolchildren in the verses of Longfellow. His opposition to British policies in North America made him one of Colonial Boston's most outspoken patriots and propagandists for the Revolutionary cause. He was a member of the Sons of Liberty, took an active part in the Boston Tea Party, and carried word of the resolve of citizens of Massachusetts to resist Great Britain from New York to Philadelphia (his bill for the trip was sold from the Elsie Sang collection at Sotheby Parke Bernet in 1978 for $70,000; it is now in the Forbes Collection). After an undistinguished military career during the war, Revere became a prosperous merchant-entrepreneur in the new Commonwealth of Massachusetts, not only crafting superb silver pieces but casting bells and domestic and marine hardware, and dealing in paper, clothing, and Sheffield plate.

Silver tankard, by Paul Revere. Boston, Massachusetts, c. 1770. Height 8½". Private collection.

This fine example of Revere's skill as a silversmith was formerly in the collection of J. P. Morgan. It was sold at Sotheby Parke Bernet, New York, on April 27, 1976, for $45,000.

Henri Matisse. *Reclining Nude, Number Two.* 1927. Bronze, length 19″. Private collection. As *Nu Couché II,* lot 6 in the auction of important nineteenth- and twentieth-century art from the collection of Mr. and Mrs. Sidney F. Brody of Los Angeles, at Sotheby Parke Bernet, New York, on October 19, 1977. One of ten bronze casts, this example brought $45,000.

Head of a Queen Mother. Benin, eighteenth century. Bronze, height 17¼″. Lot 170 in an auction of African and other tribal art held at Sotheby Parke Bernet, New York, on February 11, 1978, at 980 Madison Avenue. Consigned by the famous American clothes designer Mary McFadden of New York, this superb head brought $60,000.

Like so many other fine bronzes from the kingdom of Benin, in what is now Nigeria, this sculpture was formerly in the General Pitt-Rivers collection in Farnham, Dorset, England. After an uprising in 1897, the British, who had been in control of this part of Africa since the early years of the century, conquered Benin, sacked the city, and carried off many of the artistic treasures of the kingdom. Pitt-Rivers's holdings were all acquired at this time.

Henri Matisse. *The Lute*. 1943. Oil on canvas, 23¾ x 32″. Private collection. Lot 19 in the sale of the Brody collection at Sotheby Parke Bernet on October 19, 1977, brought $440,000.

Paintings by Henri Matisse (1869–1954) had appeared at auction in New York as early as 1922, when the Detroit Institute of Arts acquired his *Window* of 1916, at the Kelekian sale, for $2,500.

Since then, largely due to the exhibitions and publications of Alfred H. Barr, Jr., at the Museum of Modern Art in New York, Matisse has achieved an enormous reputation among American collectors.

The Lute exemplifies the artist's never-ending fascination with the female form and the power of music.

Gold and enamel box, with erotic automata and singing-bird musical movement. Swiss, c. 1800. Length 3½". Private collection. Lot 34 in the sale of important French furniture, works of art, and gold boxes from the collection of Henry Ford II, held at Sotheby Parke Bernet, New York, on February 25, 1978. The box brought $100,000.

Ceci n'est pas une pipe.

René Magritte. *The Treason of Images*. c. 1928. Oil on canvas, 23½ x 32". Private collection. As lot 70 in an auction on May 17, 1978, this famous work by the Belgian Surrealist René Magritte (1898–1967) was consigned for sale at Sotheby Parke Bernet, New York, by the painter-collector William N. Copley. At the auction, *Ceci n'est pas une pipe,* as it is often called, brought $115,000.

Prices for the best Surrealist paintings soared during the 1970s as both American and European dealers and collectors rediscovered the exciting and daring accomplishments of this controversial movement of the 1920s and 1930s.

Alfred Maurer. *Jeanne*. c. 1904. Oil on canvas, 74¾ x 39½". Private collection. Lot 36 in the sale of American paintings from the Dr. John J. McDonough collection held at Sotheby Parke Bernet, New York, on March 22, 1978. *Jeanne* sold for $115,000.

Jeanne has been identified as a model who also posed for Whistler in Paris, where Maurer (1868–1932) was studying early in the twentieth century. Within a few years, however, Maurer came under the influence of the Fauves and the Cubists, and his style changed radically from the Manet- and Chase-inspired realism of 1904, epitomized by *Jeanne*.

The conversion to modernism was not received warmly by the painter's father, Louis Maurer, a conservative artist who had worked for Currier & Ives.

The McDonough collection, dispersed in a landmark auction, had been formed within the previous twenty years, and the success of the sale helped to create a broader public awareness of the rapid advance of American painting prices.

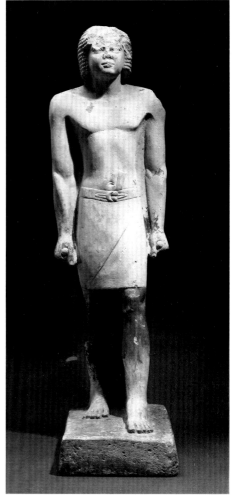

Figure of a Man. Egyptian, late Fifth Dynasty (2494–2345 B.C.). Limestone, height 31¾". Private collection. As lot 304, this important sculpture of a striding man was consigned for sale at Sotheby Parke Bernet by the Museum of Fine Arts, Boston, Massachusetts. At the auction, on December 14, 1978, this piece fetched $280,000—then a record for an ancient Egyptian work of art sold at auction—a price reflecting its distinguished provenance as well as its important size.

Frederic Edwin Church. *The Icebergs*. 1861. Oil on canvas, 64½ x 112⅜". Dallas Museum of Art. Anonymous gift. Sold as lot 34 on October 25, 1979, for $2.75 million*, the record price to date for an American painting sold at auction.

Much has been written about the discovery of the painting in 1979 in a home for boys run by the social service department of the city of Manchester, England, where it had hung since the home was the private residence of the Watkin family. It is presumed that Sir Edward William Watkin, a wealthy railroad organizer and politician, bought the painting from Church in 1863. In 1901 Watkin's son sold the family's house, "Rose Hill," complete with *The Icebergs,* to the city of Manchester.

Frederic E. Church (1826–1900) traveled to Newfoundland in 1859 to sketch icebergs near the Arctic region. He finished the large oil in his studio in 1860–61 and exhibited it at the Goupil Gallery in New York City in 1861 under the title *The North*. On April 24 of that year, the *New York Tribune* acclaimed the painting as "the most splendid work of art that has yet been produced in this country." In 1863, Church sent the painting to England for exhibition, where it remained until it was sent back to New York for sale in 1979. In October *The Icebergs* made a triumphant public reappearance in New York at a Sotheby Parke Bernet auction. During the previous decade interest in the nineteenth-century phenomenon called Luminism had been growing, and a major show of Luminist pictures was being planned by the National Gallery in Washington, D.C. Church's great canvas assumed a prominent place in the show, unexpectedly adding a new and spectacular example to a group of works that have recently claimed an important place in the history of American art.

Opposite: John Singer Sargent. *Millicent, Duchess of Sutherland*. c. 1903. Oil on canvas, 100 x 57½". Private collection. Lot 690 in the sale in New York at Sotheby Parke Bernet on June 5–9, 1979, of the contents of the house on Gramercy Park where Benjamin Sonnenberg's collection of art and antiques had delighted so many visitors, clients, and friends. The portrait brought $212,100*.

Sonnenberg, one of the original—and best—public relations men in the United States, had filled the thirty-seven rooms of his house with a splendidly wide-ranging collection of European and American paintings and drawings, English furniture, sculpture of all sorts, old and modern prints, and gleaming brass objects, forming a spectacular background for the many receptions and dinners that the Sonnenbergs hosted there. In terms of variety, choice, quality, and eccentricity, it was altogether an unforgettable collection formed by an unforgettable character.

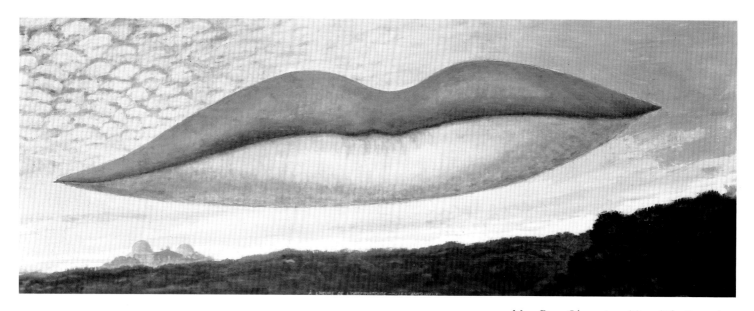

Man Ray. *Observatory Time (The Lovers)*. c. 1932–34. Oil on canvas, 39 x 98½". Private collection. Lot 33 in the auction of major Surrealist art belonging to William N. Copley, held at Sotheby Parke Bernet, New York, on November 5–6, 1979.

This picture—one of Surrealism's most famous and powerful images—sold for $825,000*.

The Copley collection's appearance at auction caused great excitement among collectors of Surrealist art all over the world. Its success was an affirmation of the strength of the art market in general, and of the market for surrealist works in particular.

Racetrack Tout, attributed to Charles Dowler. Providence, Rhode Island, c. 1870. Carved and painted wood, height 76". Private collection. Lot 194 in the sale in New York at Sotheby Parke Bernet of American folk art collected by the late Stewart E. Gregory of Wilton, Connecticut, on January 27, 1979. The figure brought $31,900*. Many significant new price levels were reached at this sale of paintings, sculptures, manufactured objects, and furniture.

In 1980, *Racetrack Tout* was resold at Sotheby Parke Bernet, fetching $58,300* at its second appearance in the salesroom as a result of increasing demand for fine examples of folk art.

1980

Ronald Reagan is elected president of the United States.

Price of silver plummets following the failure of the Hunt family's speculative attempt to control the market.

Pablo Picasso. *Saltimbanque Seated with Arms Crossed.* c. 1923. Oil on canvas, 51½ x 38¼". Bridgestone Museum of Art, Ishibashi Foundation, Tokyo. Lot 41 in the auction of Impressionist and modern art from the collection of Edgar and Bernice Chrysler Garbisch held at Sotheby Parke Bernet, New York, on May 12, 1980. The price: $3.3 million*.

Saltimbanque Seated is one of a small group of major oils that are considered to be the culmination of Picasso's classical period. This picture had formerly been in the collections of the Honorable W. Averell Harriman and Vladimir Horowitz, before being acquired by the Garbisches.

Höchst porcelain asparagus-form tureen and cover. c. 1760–65. Length 9½". Private collection. Lot 129 in the auction of French furniture, decorative arts, and ceramics from the Garbisch collection, held on May 17, 1980, at Sotheby Parke Bernet, New York, sold for $3,850*.

Mrs. Garbisch shared a love for the charming porcelains of of the eighteenth century with her sister, Thelma Chrysler Foy, whose collection was sold at Parke-Bernet in 1959.

Joseph Mallord William Turner. *Juliet and Her Nurse*. c. 1835–36. Oil on canvas, 36¼ x 48½". Amalia Lacroze de Fortabat collection, Buenos Aires, Argentina. Lot 44 in a sale at Sotheby Parke Bernet, New York, on May 29, 1980. The price was $7.04 million*—the highest price ever paid for any painting sold at auction.

The picture had been brought to America at the turn of the century by Colonel O. H. Payne, whose nephew Harry Payne Whitney and his wife, Gertrude Vanderbilt Whitney, were the parents of the consignor at the 1980 sale, Mrs. Flora Whitney Miller. Part of the proceeds from the sale of the Turner canvas went to the Whitney Museum of American Art, founded by Gertrude Vanderbilt Whitney in New York.

John Ruskin, the critic whose adverse criticism of Whistler's *Nocturne* caused that artist so much vexation (see page 132), defended *Juliet and Her Nurse* against hostile comments, helping Turner at a crucial point in his career.

Carved and painted wood plaque, attributed to John Bellamy. New England, c. 1860. Height 18¾". Private collection. Lot 875 in the sale of American furniture and decorative arts in the Garbisch collection, held by Sotheby Parke Bernet at "Pokety Farms" on May 23–25, 1980. The eagle sold for $42,900*.

An extraordinary array of Chinese export porcelain, Wedgwood and other English ceramics, and important American furniture and decorative arts were sold in situ on May 23–25, 1980, at "Pokety Farms," the country house of Colonel and Mrs. Garbisch on Lecompte Bay in Cambridge, Maryland. Thousands of visitors from near and far took advantage of the opportunity to attend an exciting pre-sale exhibition in a beautiful setting. Interest and prices were high and the results were memorable.

Chippendale mahogany blockfront kneehole desk carved with a shell motif, possibly by Edmund Townsend. Newport, Rhode Island, c. 1760–80. Height 33". Private collection. Lot 1122 in the Garbisch American furniture sale at "Pokety Farms" on May 23–25, 1980. This fine example of Newport cabinetwork brought $275,000*.

Colonel and Mrs. Garbisch had acquired the desk in 1972 at the Sotheby Parke Bernet auction of American furniture from the Lansdell Christie collection. At that time the price had been $120,000.

Aristide Maillol. *Summer.* c. 1910–11. Bronze, height 64″. Private collection. Lot 200 in an auction of paintings and sculptures held on November 5, 1981, at Sotheby Parke Bernet, New York. *Summer,* from the collection of the well-known New York dealer Sam Salz, brought $308,000*.

In 1910 Maillol (1861–1944) created a sculpture representing the goddess Pomona, which was acquired by a Russian collector. Maillol was then commissioned to make three companion bronzes: *Flora, Spring,* and, most voluptuous of the group, *Summer.*

Eleven-Headed Kwanyin (Guan Yin). Chinese, twelfth century. Wood, height 86″. The Cleveland Museum of Art, Cleveland, Ohio. Purchased from the J. H. Wade Fund. Lot 50 in an auction of Chinese ceramics, paintings, and other works of art held at Sotheby Parke Bernet, New York, on November 6, 1981. The estate of Anne Burnett Tandy of Forth Worth, Texas, was the consignor of this impressive figure of the goddess of Mercy, whose price at the sale was $187,000*.

Emerald and diamond necklace. c. 1930. Private collection. On April 14, 1981, lot 37 in a Sotheby Parke Bernet, New York, auction of important precious-stone jewelry from the estate of Mrs. Georges Lurcy, of High Point, North Carolina, sold for $154,000*.

Mrs. Lurcy was the widow of Georges Lurcy, whose collection was sold at Parke-Bernet in 1957.

Pablo Picasso. *Yo, Picasso*. 1901. Oil on canvas, 29 x 23¾". Private collection. Lot 536 in an auction at Sotheby Parke Bernet, New York, on May 21, 1981, sold for $5.83 million*.

This brilliant early self-portrait, done by Picasso (1881–1973) when he was only twenty years old, captures perfectly the exuberance and the confident personality of a great twentieth-century artist whose *oeuvre* covers virtually every style and medium known.

Silver two-handled bowl, by Benjamin Wynkoop. New York, probably 1707. Diameter 8″. Private collection. Lot 188 in a sale of American silver held on November 16, 1981, at Sotheby Parke Bernet, New York, fetched $121,000*.

Fewer than twenty such two-handled, paneled bowls, which show the persistence of old Dutch silversmithing traditions in New York, are known to exist. They were used for ceremonial drinking and toasting at formal occasions such as weddings, anniversaries, and christenings, when they were passed round for the guests to share a strong punch. This example was made by Wynkoop (1675–1728) for Nicholas Roosevelt and his wife, Hillitje, whose initials are on the cup. They celebrated the twenty-fifth anniversary of their wedding in 1707, the likely date of the piece.

1982

Argentine troops seize the Falkland Islands.

Antinuclear controversy rages in the United States and Europe; huge peace rallies are held in major cities.

Porcelain shell-form sweetmeat stand, by Bonnin & Morris. Philadelphia, c. 1771–72. Height 5″. Private collection. Lot 331 in a sale of Americana held at Sotheby Parke Bernet, New York, on January 27–30, 1982. The price: $66,000*.

This charming candy dish was produced by America's first and only porcelain factory active in the eighteenth century. Only a few pieces have survived to indicate the nature of the wares produced by Bonnin & Morris. The factory was put out of business within two years of its beginning, in 1770, by a flood of cheap imports.

Sancai ("three-color") glazed pottery figure of a court lady. Chinese, Tang Dynasty (618–907). Height 16″. Private collection. Lot 57 in the auction of important Chinese ceramics, bronzes, and works of art from the collection of Captain S. N. Ferris Luboshez, held at Sotheby Parke Bernet, New York, on November 18, 1982, sold for $198,000*.

Molded and gilt copper Statue of Liberty weathervane, by J. L. Motti Ironworks. New York or Chicago, late nineteenth century. Private collection. Lot 8 in the sale of American folk art collected by Thomas G. Rizzo of New York held on April 29, 1982, at Sotheby Parke Bernet, New York. The vane brought $82,500*.

American weathervanes climbed especially dramatically in price following the S. E. Gregory sale in 1979.

Step-cut emerald ring by Cartier. Private collection. Lot 302 in the sale of precious-stone jewelry held on April 20, 1983, at Sotheby Parke Bernet, New York. The 14.24-carat emerald was consigned by the estate of Gladys Letts Pollock of Los Angeles and brought $495,000*.

Fine colored stones such as rubies, emeralds, and sapphires rose swiftly in price during the 1970s and 1980s because of intense international competition at major auctions for the best pieces.

Hilaire Germain Edgar Degas. *L'Attente (Waiting).* c. 1882. Pastel on paper, 19 x 24″. Collections of the J. Paul Getty Museum, Malibu, California, and the Norton Simon Museum, Pasadena, California. Lot 8 in the sale of Impressionist paintings and drawings from the estate of Doris D. Havemeyer held at Sotheby Parke Bernet, New York, on May 16, 1983, *L'Attente* brought $3.74 million*.

In the shifting patterns of ballet and in the complicated postures of the ballerinas who dedicate their lives to it Degas found an endless source of visual stimulation. Mrs. H. O. Havemeyer, whose husband acquired *L'Attente* in 1895 from Degas's dealer, Paul Durand-Ruel, recalled in her memoirs that the pastel "is rather somber in tone and subject, but is the perfection of art in every detail."

Mernepthah, Royal Scribe and Charioteer. Egyptian, reign of Rameses II (1304–1237 B.C.). Granite, height 31″. Private collection. Lot 30 in an antiquities sale held at Sotheby Parke Bernet, New York, on June 10–11, 1983. The price: $375,100*.

This impressive and documentary sculpture, inscribed with the sitter's name and other details of his life, career, and death, was presented in 1887 to the Chautauqua Institution, an American educational organization headquartered in Chautauqua, New York, by the Egyptian Exploration Fund shortly after its discovery at Nebesheh, in Egypt, by Sir W. M. Flinders Petrie.

After years of neglect, the statue was found in 1983 languishing in an unused railroad station at Chautauqua. The price achieved at the sale was the highest ever fetched for an Egyptian antiquity at auction.

Charles Sheeler. *Classic Landscape*. 1931. Oil on canvas, 25 x 32¼". Lot 201 in an American paintings sale held at Sotheby Parke Bernet, New York, on June 2, 1983. The price was $2,057,000*.

The painting, depicting the Ford Motor Company plant at River Rouge, near Detroit, Michigan, is in Sheeler's distinctive, Precisionist manner. An important photographer as well as a painter of note, Sheeler (1883–1965) completed a series of photographs of the plant three years earlier that are very similar in feeling to the later series of paintings to which this belongs. *Classic Landscape* was formerly in the collection of Edsel Ford and was consigned by Detroit's Edsel and Eleanor Ford House.

Opposite: Louis XIV ormolu-mounted small writing table with Boúlle marquetry. French, early eighteenth century. Height 30¼". Private collection. Lot 207 in a French furniture sale held on May 7, 1983, at Sotheby Parke Bernet, New York, brought $914,650*.

Boulle marquetry is the term generally used to describe a distinctive brass and tortoise-shell decorative veneer perfected in France by André-Charles Boulle (1642–1732), the first great French *ébéniste*. About 1715 Boulle turned over the family business to his sons, who continued his traditions of artisanry.

A virtually identical *bureau plat* with the brass and tortoise-shell marquetry reversed (thus, probably made at the same time) is in the Musée Condé at Chantilly, France.

Notes and Sources

A note on auction prices: Prior to 1979 no additional premium was added by Sotheby Parke Bernet and its predecessor firms to the "hammer price," the buyer's final bid. Beginning in the 1930s, however, New York City and New York State sales taxes were added to the hammer price, and from World War II into the 1950s a luxury tax was payable on such items as jewels, furs, gold, and silver.

Starting with sales held in New York after January 1, 1979, Sotheby Parke Bernet joined the ranks of all other international auction rooms in adding a 10 percent "buyer's premium" to the hammer price. In this book, when the price paid for an object includes the 10 percent buyer's premium, that price is followed by an asterisk.

1885: Lee Hollister Sturges, *Jules Breton and the French Rural Tradition,* 1982, p. 96, no. 42, illus. p. 43. This catalogue of a recent exhibition at the Joslyn Art Museum, Omaha, Nebraska, includes an essay by Madeleine Fidell-Beaufort, "Jules Breton in America: Collecting in the 19th Century," which provides much useful information about the early buyers of Breton's pictures, who usually made their purchases through the dealer Samuel Putnam Avery (1822–1904) and his Paris-based associate, George A. Lucas (1824–1909).

The following year, at the Mary Jane Morgan sale, Breton's *Communicants* fetched $45,000.

1886: On Vibert's *Missionary's Adventures,* see: Charles Sterling and Margaretta M. Salinger, *French Paintings: A Catalogue of the Collection of the Metropolitan Museum of Art,* vol. 2, 1966, pp. 197–98, illus.; and S. N. Behrman, *Duveen,* 1952, pp. 195–96.

The story of the American Art Association's Impressionist exhibition has been recounted in most of the standard books on the movement and its individual exponents, often with mistakes as to the precise date, location, success, and other particulars of the show. Works by certain of the Impressionists had been included in one or two mixed exhibitions held in the United States, but the show at the American Art Association in 1886 was the first devoted solely to this school of painting. See: *America and Europe: A Century of Modern Masters from the Thyssen-Bornemisza Collection,* 1979, p. 132, no. 2.

1887: On Powers's *Greek Slave,* see: William H. Gerdts, *American Neo-Classic Sculpture: The Marble Resurrection,* 1973, pp. 52–55. Prince Anatole Demidoff (1812–1870) was son of the fabulously wealthy Russian expatriate Count Nikolai Demidoff (1773–1828), who built the palace of San Donato near Florence, where the family art collections were displayed. In 1870, after Prince Demidoff's death, ten auctions were held in Paris to disperse the bulk of the collection—one of the greatest series of auction sales of the possessions of a single owner ever held. In 1880 a second series of sales took place, on the premises of San Donato Palace.

On Bonheur's *Horse Fair* and Meissonier's *Friedland,* see: Charles Sterling and Margaretta M. Salinger, *French Paintings: A Catalogue of the Collection of the Metropolitan Museum of Art,* vol. 2, 1966, pp. 152–54, 161–64, illus.

1889: The circumstances surrounding the sale of the Duque de Durcal's pictures remain unclear. Apparently, they were consigned to the American Art Association by the owner's agent, Mr. S. Montgomery Roosevelt, a cousin of Theodore Roosevelt and a part-time art dealer. The paintings' attributions were seriously questioned by the *New York Tribune,* and the owner, a young Spanish nobleman who had crossed the Atlantic to attend the sale, was aggrieved and insulted by the reception given his family heirlooms. The date of the auction was postponed from April 5–6 to April 10–11, and Durcal convinced the auctioneer, Thomas Kirby, to announce the minimum price acceptable to the seller as each lot was put up. The results amounted to a fiasco, for very few pictures were sold, either at the New York auction or at a second sale in Paris in 1890. See: Wesley

Towner, *The Elegant Auctioneers,* 1970, pp. 147–48.

On van der Weyden's *Saint Luke Painting the Virgin,* see: *Flanders in the Fifteenth Century: Art and Civilization,* catalogue of an exhibition held at the Detroit Institute of Arts, 1960, pp. 75–80, illus.

1889/90: On the sojourn of Millet's *Angelus* in New York, see: Laura Meixner, *An International Episode: Millet, Monet, and Their North American Contemporaries,* catalogue of an exhibition circulated by the Dixon Gallery and Gardens, Memphis, Tennessee, 1982, p. 81 f.

Henry James's remarks on the Barye cult may be found in the *New York Tribune,* December 25, 1875.

1891: *Paris–New York: A Continuing Romance,* catalogue of the centenary exhibition of the Wildenstein Gallery, 1977, p. 60, no. 72.

1893: Peter Hassrick, *Frederic Remington: Paintings, Drawings, and Sculpture in the Amon Carter Museum and the Sid W. Richardson Foundation Collections,* 1973, pp. 35–36.

1894: *The Other Nineteenth Century: Paintings and Sculpture in the Collection of Mr. and Mrs. Joseph M. Tanenbaum,* 1978, pp. 184, 188–89, no. 67. Although the provenance listed in this book does not mention Seney as a former owner, the size, subject, and description of *Without Dowry* make it virtually certain that the picture was once in Seney's collection of modern pictures.

1895: Daniel Wildenstein, *Claude Monet: Biographie et catalogue raisonné,* vol. 1, 1974, no. 1212.

1896: Charles Sterling and Margaretta M. Salinger, *French Paintings: A Catalogue of the Collection of the Metropolitan Museum of Art,* vol. 2, 1966, pp. 78, 82–83, 94–95, 97, illus.

1897: A revival of interest in this group of painters is evidenced by a recent exhibition with its splendid catalogue, *The Hague School: Dutch Masters of the 19th Century,* Paris, London, and the Hague, 1983.

1898: John I. H. Baur, *Theodore Robinson,* catalogue of an exhibition at the Brooklyn Museum, 1946, p. 71, no. 169. It should be reiterated that there were only ninety-four paintings and watercolors in Theodore Robinson's estate sale of 1898. Both signed and unsigned works were listed, but no estate stamp or facsimile signature was affixed to the unsigned examples. Thus, the numerous oil sketches that have appeared on the market from time to time stamped "Th. Robinson Sale" were not included in the auction of Robinson's estate in 1898. Their mysterious origin remains to be identified conclusively.

1899: Thomas B. Clarke's papers are now in the Archives of American Art. The American Art Association–Anderson Galleries, Inc., held an auction of Clarke's effects in 1931, after his death the previous year.

1900: Abram Lerner, ed., *The Hirshhorn Museum and Sculpture Garden, Smithsonian Institution,* 1974, p. 666, fig. 109. In the Evans sale catalogue, a picture of the same size as *The Three Trees* called *Evening on the Sound* is listed. The description suggests it was indeed *The Three Trees,* though the lighthouse is described as being on the right. Since the picture was not illustrated in the catalogue, it is possible that the cataloguer was in error on this point.

1901: The first "all photography" sale at Parke-Bernet Galleries—that of the Will Weisberg collection in 1967—was held at PB Eighty-Four, Parke-Bernet's subsidiary salesroom at 171 East Eighty-fourth Street.

1902: On Courbet's *Trellis,* see: *The Toledo Museum of Art: European Paintings,* 1976, pp. 42–43, plate 218.

On Manet's *Smoker,* see: Denis Rouart and Daniel Wildenstein, *Edouard Manet: Catalogue raisonné,* 1975, vol. 1, p. 110, no. 112, illus. p. 111.

1903: An up-to-date study of the English academic painter Sir Lawrence Alma-Tadema is: Vern G. Swenson, *Alma-Tadema,* 1977, p. 26.

On *Madonna in a Niche,* see: John Pope-Hennessy, *Luca Della Robbia,* 1980, p. 255, no. 40, plate XXIX.

1904: On *The Titan's Goblet,* see: Howard S. Merritt, *Thomas Cole,* 1969, pp. 29–30. For a different interpretation of the picture's symbolism, see: Diana Strazdes, "The Titan's Goblet," in Theodore E. Stebbins et al., *A New World: Masterpieces of American Painting, 1760–1910,* 1983, p. 224, no. 24, illus. p. 67.

1905: On *Arab Fantasia,* see: *L'opera pittorica completa di Delacroix (Classici dell' Arte* series, no. 57), 1972, pp. 100–101, no. 244.

1906: Horst Gerson, *Rembrandt Paintings,* 1968, pp. 294, 495, fig. 179. Petronella Buys's husband, Philips Lucasz., Councillor of the East India Company, was also painted by Rembrandt in 1635. His portrait now hangs in the National Gallery, London.

1907: On *Diana of the Tower,* see: John H. Dryfhout, *The Work of Augustus Saint-Gaudens,* 1982, p. 155, cat. no. 121, illus. Saint-Gaudens died in August 1907, and a memorial service was held for him at Mendelssohn Hall on March 2, 1908.

On *Pegasus,* see: Lloyd Goodrich, *Albert P. Ryder,* 1959, fig. 11.

1908: A *Catalogue of the Collection of American Paintings in the Corcoran Gallery of Art,* vol. 1, 1966, p. 127, illus. See also: Gordon Hendricks, *Albert Bierstadt: Painter of the American West,* 1974, pp. 282–91, fig. 205.

1909: On Chase's *Kimono,* see: *America and Europe: A Century of Modern Masters from the Thyssen-Bornemisza Collection,* 1979, p. 136, no. 12, illus. p. 35.

On Lefebvre's *Language of the Fan,* see: Eric M. Zafran, *French Salon Paintings from Southern Collections,* 1983, pp. 138–39, illus.

For a discussion of Japanese influence on Western art, see: Edward W. Said, *Orientalism,* 1978.

1910: On Gérôme's *Pygmalion and Galatea,* see: Charles Sterling and Margaretta M. Salinger, *French Paintings: A Catalogue of the Collection of the Metropolitan Museum of Art,* vol. 2, 1966, pp. 172–78, illus.

1911: On Pesellino's *Madonna and Child with Saint John,* see: *The Toledo Museum of Art: European Paintings,* 1976, pp. 124–25, colorplate I.

On the sale of Hoe's Gutenberg Bible, see: Edward Wolf II, with John F. Fleming, *Rosenbach,* 1960, p. 72.

1912: Brenda Auslander, "A Still Life by Jan Brueghel the Elder," in *Art at Auction: The Year at Sotheby Parke Bernet, 1978–79,* 1979, pp. 20–21.

1913: On Daumier's *Third-Class Carriage,* see: Charles Sterling and Margaretta M. Salinger, *French Paintings: A Catalogue of the Collection of the Metropolitan Museum of Art,* vol. 2, 1966, pp. 37–39, illus. See also: Calvin Tompkins, *Merchants and Masterpieces: The Story of the Metropolitan Museum of Art,* 1970, p. 208. Louisine Havemeyer's autobiography is: *Sixteen to Sixty: Memoirs of a Collector,* 1961.

1914: Jerry E. Patterson, "'Shine, Mister?'—The Urchin Art of J. G. Brown," in *Auction,* June 1971, pp. 38–41.

1916: On the Florentine bowl, see: Joseph J. Kuntz, "The Medici Bowl from Seton College," in *Art at Auction: The Year at Sotheby Parke Bernet, 1973-74,* 1974, pp. 374–76. This is actually a piece of soft-paste porcelain, so called to distinguish it from the true porcelain first produced in Europe at Meissen, Germany, in the eighteenth century, after the discovery of kaolin clay, the essential ingredient.

1917: On Chase's *The Artist's Daughter in Her Mother's Dress,* see: Abram Lerner, ed., *The Hirshhorn Museum and Sculpture Garden, Smithsonian Institution,* 1974, p. 673, fig. 78.

On Eakins's *Sailing,* see: Lloyd Goodrich, *Thomas Eakins,* 1982, vol. 1, p. 106, fig. 43; vol. 2, p. 220.

On *Pleasure Boats at Argenteuil,* see: Daniel Wildenstein, *Claude Monet: Biographie et catalogue raisonné,* vol. 1, 1974, p. 272, no. 368.

1918: On Gris's *Still Life with Playing Cards,* see: Douglas Cooper, *Juan Gris: Catalogue raisonné de l'oeuvre peint, établi avec la collaboration de Margaret Potter,* 1977, vol. 1, no. 189. Cooper does not mention the Anderson Galleries' auction, but since size, date, first owner, and subject are the same, item number 189 in his catalogue is almost certainly identical with lot 94-B in the Anderson sale of 1918. Léonce Alexandre Rosenberg, as he was referred to in the sale catalogue, is usually called simply Léonce Rosenberg. He was the brother of another famous art dealer, Paul Rosenberg, and the uncle of Alexandre Rosenberg, who is today a leading art dealer in New York City.

On Donatello's *Virgin and Child with Two Angels,* see: John Pope-Hennessy, "A Terracotta 'Madonna' by Donatello," in *Burlington Magazine,* February 1983, pp. 83–84, plate 1.

1919: Captain De Lamar bought the Great Mosque Carpet of Ardebil for $27,000 at the 1910 Yerkes auction. Joseph Duveen paid $57,000 for it at the De Lamar auction (he is quoted as having said he was prepared to go to $250,000), and J. Paul Getty acquired it from Duveen in 1938 for $70,000—much less than Duveen had asked for it before the Depression lowered the prices for such carpets. Getty later bequeathed the rug to the Los Angeles County Museum. See: J. Paul Getty, *As I See It,* 1976, p. 273.

On the English petit-point embroidery, see: Yvonne Hackenbroch, *English and Other Needlework Tapestries and Textiles in the Irwin Untermyer Collection* (Metropolitan Museum of Art), 1960, p. 18, fig. 43, plate 27.

1921: On the stained glass from Soissons Cathedral, see: Jane Hayward and Walter Cahn, *Radiance and Reflection: Medieval Art from the Pitcairn Collection* (Metropolitan Museum of Art), 1982, pp. 36–38, 140, 149–52, frontispiece in color.

On *The Aero,* see: Barbara Haskell, *Marsden Hartley,* 1980, pp. 61–62, 214.

On the French-style furniture from Philadelphia, see the catalogue of the 1976 Philadelphia Museum exhibition: *Philadelphia: Three Centuries of American Art,* pp. 205–6, no. 170.

On Degas's *Madame René De Gas,* see: John Walker, *The National Gallery of Art, Washington,* 1975, p. 476, no. 706.

1925: On *Maria and Her Dog Silvio,* see: Benedict Nicolson, *Joseph Wright of Derby: Painter of Light,* 1968, vol. 1, p. 246, no. 237 (as *Maria, from Sterne*). Maria, a character who first appeared in Laurence Sterne's *Tristram Shandy,* was abandoned by her lover and her goat in that novel. In Sterne's last book, *Sentimental Journey,* her only companion is her pet dog, Silvio.

On Corot's *Saint Sebastian Tended by the Holy Women,* see: Eric M. Zafran, *French Salon Paintings from Southern Collections,* 1982, p. 80, no. 20.

1926: For Bishop's reactions to the Leverhulme sale, see: Wesley Towner, *The Elegant Auctioneers,* 1970, pp. 411–12.

1927: B. L. Reid, *The Man from New York: John Quinn and His Friends,* 1968. See also: Henry McBride, *The Flow of Art,* 1975, which includes his *Dial* pieces for February and March 1926.

On Kuhn's *Tragic Comedians,* see: Abram Lerner, ed., *The Hirshhorn Museum and Sculpture Garden, Smithsonian Institution,* 1974, p. 709, fig. 305.

On Gwen John's *Woman Reading at a Window,* see the catalogue of the Gwen John retrospective exhibition held at Davis & Long Company, New York, in 1975, p. 14, no. 4.

1928: Ronald Freyburger, "The Judge Elbert H. Gary Sale," *Auction,* June 1969, pp. 10–13.

1929: Wendy Cooper, *In Praise of America,* 1980 (published in conjunction with an exhibition of American decorative arts at the National Gallery of Art, Washington, D.C.); and, by the same author, "A Historic Event: The 1929 Girl Scout Loan Exhibition," *American Art Journal,* Winter 1980, pp. 28–40. See also: Jerry E. Patterson, "The Reifsnyder Collection," *Auction,* April 1968, pp. 5–6.

On the Chippendale "sample" armchairs, see: *Philadelphia: Three Centuries of American Art,* catalogue of an exhibition at the Philadelphia Museum of Art, 1976, pp. 112–13, no. 89.

1930: On *Girl Arranging Her Hair,* see: Frank Getlein, *Mary Cassatt: Paintings and Prints,* 1980, pp. 58–59.

1931: On the Queen Anne long-case clock, see: Yvonne Hackenbroch, *English Furniture . . . in the Irwin Untermyer Collection* (Metropolitan Museum of Art), 1958, p. 9, fig. 18, plate 12.

1932: On the Tickhill Psalter, see: Edward Wolf II, with John F. Fleming, *Rosenbach,* 1960, pp. 365–67.

On Boucher's *Venus Consoling Love,* see: John Walker, *The National Gallery of Art, Washington,* 1975, pp. 334–35, no. 447.

1933: On Sorolla's *The Wounded Foot,* see: J. Paul Getty, *As I See It,* 1976, p. 267.

On Ryan's patronage of Rodin, see: Clare Vincent, "Rodin at the Metropolitan Museum of Art: A History of the Collection," *Bulletin of the Metropolitan Museum of Art,* Spring 1981.

On Laurana's *Princess of the House of Aragon,* see: John Walker, *The National Gallery of Art, Washington,* 1975, p. 633, no. 980.

1935: On the cassone, see: *Columbus Museum of Art: Catalogue of the Collection,* 1978, p. 119, where it is noted that Bishop had acquired the chest at the Luigi Grassi auction (American Art Association, January 20, 1927, lot 543) for $7,500, and that the buyer at the Bishop auction was William Randolph Hearst.

1936: On the Chippendale chair, see: Yvonne Hackenbroch, *English Furniture . . . in the Irwin Untermyer Collection* (Metropolitan Museum of Art), 1958, p. 29, figs. 131, 132, plates 104, 105.

On Trumbull's miniature portrait of Ceracchi, see: Stuart P. Feld and Albert Ten Eyck Gardner, *American Paintings in the Metropolitan Museum of Art,* vol. 1, 1965, p. 105, illus.

1937: On Coney's Monteith bowl, see: Martha Gandy Fales, *Early American Silver,* rev. ed., 1973, pp. 13–14, fig. 14.

1940: On *Nocturne in Black and Gold,* see: Denys Sutton, *James McNeill Whistler: Paintings, Etchings, Pastels, and Watercolors,* 1966, p. 191, no. 70. See also: Andrew McLaren Young, Margaret MacDonald Spencer, and Robin Spencer, *The Paintings of James McNeill Whistler,* 1980, vol. 1, p. 97, no. 170, plates 153, 403 (vol. 2).

1941: On the Rubens Vase, see: Michael Jaffe, *Rubens and Italy,* 1977, p. 84. The Hamilton Palace sales took place in June and July 1882, in London, dispersing the large and important collection of the twelfth duke of Hamilton.

On Blake's *The Great Red Dragon,* see: Martin Butlin, *The Paintings and Drawings of William Blake,* 1981, no. 520, plate 581.

1942: On the press-cupboard, see: Yvonne Hackenbroch, *English Furniture . . . in the Irwin Untermyer Collection* (Metropolitan Museum of Art), 1958, p. 65, fig. 313, plate 271.

On *Raphael and the Fornarina,* see: Georges Wildenstein, *Ingres,* 2d rev. ed., 1956, p. 11, no. 231.

1944: On Philippe de Champaigne's portrait of Charles II, see: *The Cleveland Museum of Art: Catalogue of Paintings. Part III: European Paintings of the 16th, 17th, and 18th Centuries,* 1982, p. 57, no. 24. When the picture was auctioned in Paris in 1903, by a descendant of the owner of the Château de Saint Germain, it was catalogued as *James II,* a portrait by Sir Peter Lely. The correct subject and attribution were determined by Charles Sterling as late as 1944, when the painting was sold at Parke-Bernet Galleries.

On the miniature sedan chair, see: Hermione Waterfield and Christopher Forbes, *Fabergé Imperial Eggs and Other Fantasies,* 1978, p. 48, illus. fig. 58.

1947: On the Bay Psalm Book sale, see: Edward Wolf II, with John F. Fleming, *Rosenbach,* 1960.

1948: On *The Birthplace of Herbert Hoover,* see: James Dennis, *Grant Wood,* 1975, p. 240.

1950: On *Mademoiselle Pogany,* see: Sidney Geist, *Brancusi: A Study of the Sculpture,* 1983, pp. 190–91.

1951: On *Still Life: A Kitchen Table with Skate,* see: Pierre Rosenberg, *Chardin,* 1979, pp. 162–63.

On *Male Saint with a Book,* see: Gianfranco Contini and Maria Cristina Gozzoli, *L'opera completa di Simone Martini (Classici dell' Arte* series), 1970, p. 88, no. 8.

1954: On Raeburn's *Portrait of Mrs. Robertson Williamson,* see: *Columbus Museum of Art: Catalogue of the Collection,* 1978, p. 97. See also: *Connoisseur,* vol. 77, no. 305 (January 1927), p. 45.

On *Benjamin and Eleanor Ridgely Laming,* see: Charles Coleman Sellers, *Charles Willson Peale,* 1969, p. 321, illus.

1955: On the Logan Tankard, see: *Philadelphia: Three Centuries of American Art,* catalogue of an exhibition at the Philadelphia Museum of Art, 1976, p. 17, no. 12.

1956: Henry Stevens, *Recollections of James Lenox,* ed. and rev. by V. H. Paltsits, 1951. See especially Chapter VI, "Mr. Lenox Buys a Turner." See also: Martin Butlin and Evelyn Joll, *The Paintings of J.M.W. Turner,* 1977, p. 189, no. 347, plate 329.

1963: On *The Merry Lute Player,* see: W. R. Valentiner, *Frans Hals Paintings in America,* 1936, no. 20.

1964: Cleve Gary, ed., *David Smith by David Smith,* 1968, p. 77.

1965: On the Fabergé clock, see: Hermione Waterfield and Christopher Forbes, *Fabergé Imperial Eggs and Other Fantasies,* 1978, pp. 30–32, plate 9.

1968: Gordon Nowell-Usticke's book is: *Rembrandt's Etchings: States and Values,* 1967.

1969: On Harnett's painting, see: Alfred Frankenstein, "Mr. Hulings' Rack Picture," *Auction,* February 1969, pp. 6–9.

1970: On Watteau's *Couple Seated on a Bank,* see: *The Armand Hammer Collection,* ed. John Walker, 1980, p. 208, plate 78.

1972: On *Reclining Figure,* see: John Hedgecoe and Henry Moore, *Henry Moore,* 1968, p. 171, illus. p. 170.

1974: The story of how the Chippendale chairs left Philadelphia and found their way to England, only to be "discovered" at Sotheby's, has been told in a book by David Loughlin, *The Case of Major Fanshaw's Chairs,* 1978. See also: Lita Solis-Cohen, "General John Cadwalader's 'Hairy-paw-foot' Furniture," in *Art at Auction: The Year at Sotheby's, 1982–83,* 1983, pp. 254–59.

1975: On *Alpine Mastiffs Reanimating a Distressed Traveler,* see: Richard Ormond, *Sir Edwin Landseer,* 1981, pp. 50–51, where the scene is identified as being near the famed Hospice of Saint Bernard in the Swiss Alps and the dogs as "wonderfully observed, with huge bodies and slobbering jaws...[they] dominate the composition"; fig. 113.

1979: On Church's *Icebergs,* see: John Wilmerding, *American Light: The Luminist Movement, 1850–1875,* catalogue of an exhibition at the National Gallery of Art, Washington, D.C., 1980.

1980: Juliet and Her Nurse is discussed at length in the most complete and up-to-date work on the artist, Martin Butlin and Evelyn Joll's *The Paintings of J.M.W. Turner,* 1977, pp. 195–96, no. 365, plate 343.

1981: On *Summer,* see: *Hommage à Aristide Maillol,* centennial exhibition catalogue of the Musée National d'Art Moderne, Paris, 1961, pp. 11–12.
On the Wynkoop bowl, see: Martha Gandy Fales, *Early American Silver,* rev. ed., 1973, pp. 134–35, fig. 132.

1983: For an account of how Mr. and Mrs. Havemeyer acquired *L'Attente* by Degas, see: Louisine W. Havemeyer, *Sixteen to Sixty: Memoirs of a Collector,* 1961, pp. 246, 258.

General Bibliography

The sales catalogues published by Sotheby Parke Bernet and its predecessor firms from 1885 onward have been the principal source for all the information in this book. These catalogues are available in many public libraries. Since 1964, when Sotheby's, London, merged with Parke-Bernet Galleries, the firm has published an annual review entitled *The Ivory Hammer* until 1967 and *Art at Auction* thereafter. These I have relied on for many details. The following works were also indispensable:

HERRMANN, FRANK. *Sotheby's: Portrait of an Auction House.* London: Chatto & Windus, 1980.

LANCOUR, HAROLD, comp. "American Art Auction Catalogues, 1785–1942: A Union List." New York: New York Public Library, 1943.

TOWNER, WESLEY. *The Elegant Auctioneers.* New York: Hill & Wang, 1970.

A Note on Prices through the Years

Currency fluctuations, wars, industrial development, and changes in technology and productivity make it virtually impossible to compare the prices paid for works of art at various times between 1883 and 1983. We know instinctively, of course, that $20,000 paid for a painting in 1900 or 1950 means something quite different from $20,000 paid for a painting in 1970 or 1980. But the exact difference is difficult to measure.

In order to give a constant measure of value throughout the time span of this book, I have chosen three separate indices from the *Statistical Abstract of the United States,* published by the Bureau of Labor Statistics: (1) the New York price of an ounce of silver (which, unlike gold, has no long history of controlled prices); (2) the American price of a bushel of wheat; (3) the Consumer Price Index measured against the base year of 1967 (i.e., 1967 = 100); figures below 100 indicate greater purchasing power of the dollar and figures above 100 indicate lesser purchasing power of the dollar.

Calendar year	Value of one bushel of wheat in dollars	Value of one ounce of silver in dollars	Consumer Price Index
1880	1.05–1.25	1.15	29
1890	.86– .89	1.04	27
1900	.70	.61	25
1910	1.09	.53	28
1920	2.45	1.00	60
1930	.90	.38	50
1940	.87	.34	42
1950	1.66	.74	72
1960	1.99	.91	89
1970	1.48	1.77	116
1980	4.85	20.00*	246
1981	4.86	10.52	272
1982	4.46	8.00	297

Note: Figures have been rounded off and are approximate.
*Speculation created an extremely high price temporarily.

Directory of Sotheby's Predecessor Firms in America

American Art Association

1883–1922: 6–8 East 23rd Street

James F. Sutton, Partner
R. Austin Robertson, Partner
Thomas E. Kirby, Partner
·(after 1913, Senior Partner, Chairman)

1922–1929: 30 East 57th Street
Cortlandt F. Bishop, Chairman
Hiram H. Parke, President

John Anderson, Jr. (book auctions)

1900–1901: 34 West 30th Street
1901–1903: 20 West 30th Street
1903: 91 Fifth Avenue

John Anderson, Jr., founder

Anderson Auction Company

1903–1908: 5 West 29th Street
John Anderson, Jr., President

1908–1911: 12 West 46th Street
Emory S. Turner, President

1912–1915: 16 East 40th Street
Emory S. Turner, President

Anderson Galleries

1915–1917: 16 East 40th Street
Mitchell Kennerly, President

1917–1929: 489 Park Avenue
Mitchell Kennerly, President

Anderson Galleries merged with American Art Association 1929

American Art Association–Anderson Galleries

1929–1939: 30 East 57th Street

Cortlandt F. Bishop, Chairman 1929–35
R. Milton Mitchell, President 1929–33
Hiram H. Parke, President 1933–37
Milton Logan, President 1937–39

Parke-Bernet Galleries

1937–1939: 742 Fifth Avenue

Hiram H. Parke, President
Otto Bernet, Vice President
Arthur Swann, Vice President

1939-1949: 30 East 57th Street

Hiram H. Parke, President
Otto Bernet, Vice President (died 1945)

1949: 110 East 58th Street (temporary galleries)

1949–1964: 980 Madison Avenue

Leslie A. Hyam, President 1950–63
Louis J. Marion, President 1963–64

Parke-Bernet Galleries, affiliated with Sotheby & Co., London

1964–1972: 980 Madison Avenue

Louis J. Marion, President 1964–65
Peregrine M.P.H. Pollen, President 1965–72

Sotheby Parke Bernet

1972–1982: 980 Madison Avenue

Peter C. Wilson, Chairman 1972–79
John L. Marion, President 1972–

1982–1984: 72nd Street and York Avenue
(1334 York Avenue)

John L. Marion, Chairman and President

Sotheby's

1984–: 72nd Street and York Avenue
(1334 York Avenue)

A. Alfred Taubman,
Group Chairman and Chief Executive Officer
John L. Marion,
Chairman and President (America)

Index

Page numbers in *italic* type refer to illustrations.